Unfinished Business

Sermons by Ziegler Award Preachers

William C. Coleman, Editor

Unfinished Business:
Sermons by Ziegler Award Preachers

Published by Boston Wesleyan Press
An Imprint of the Boston Wesleyan Association

Book & Cover Design by Graphic Details, Inc.
Portsmouth, New Hampshire

First Edition, June 2001

ISBN: 0-9711146-0-9

Address inquiries to:
BW Press
P.O. Box 458
North Berwick, ME 03906
Printed in the United States of America

Acknowledgments

Rev. Wilbur Ziegler, whose sense of integrity and justice are among his many virtues, is an inspiration to many of us in New England United Methodism. I admire and cherish his influence and courage. While disease now clouds his mind so that he will not know my gratitude, I thank him for his witness, nevertheless.

Thank you to the 15 Ziegler Preaching Award colleagues who willingly supported this project by sending me several of their sermons for inclusion in this book. Their sermon gifts are labors of love. They readily agreed that should any royalties accrue from this volume, they will be given to the New England Conference of the United Methodist Church, to be divided evenly between the Church and Society Committee and the Congregational Development Committee.

Rev. Dr. Thomas Gallen, a sometime collector of sundry items, had somehow acquired a dozen sermons on tape by the Rev. Ziegler. I appreciate his gracious willingness to lend them to me. Two sermons from that collection are included in this volume.

While I bear responsibility for any textual errors, there would be many more had not Rev. Dr. John Ward and Rev. Dr. Paul Deats given the text a thorough scouring. Both are emeriti faculty of the Boston University School of Theology. Perhaps it felt to them as though they were back at BU reading theses and term papers looking for errors in spelling, punctuation and sentence construction. In any case, thank you for your sharp eyes, tenacity and constructive criticism.

The members and staff of the Boston Wesleyan Association, especially Stephen Swecker, editor of *Zion's Herald*, made this project come to completion. They took a risk by agreeing to publish this, their first book. I wish them well in future publications.

Finally, my deep appreciation to my spouse, Dr. Roslyn Coleman, for her abiding encouragement. She willingly read and made corrections to the text. Most importantly, however, she brought me into the 21st century magic of computer skills and hardware gadgets that are truly labor saving and fun.

Contents

Ziegler Preaching Award Recipients

1981	Rev. T. Landon Lindsay
1982	Rev. Carlton R. Daley
1983	Rev. Harold R. Hodgson
1984	Rev. William M. (Scott) Campbell
1985	Rev. Richard E. Black
1986	Rev. Frances P. Swartz
1987	Rev. Dr. David A. Purdy
1988	Rev. Dr. Donald A. Rudalevige
1989	Rev. Shirley S. Hoover
1990	Rev. Dr. William C. Coleman
1991	Rev. Dr. Robert Alan Moore
1992	Rev. Dr. Mark A. Fowler
1993	Rev. David C. Hollenbeck
1994	Rev. Jonathan R. Almond
1995	Rev. David C. Myers
1996	Rev. Dr. Robert O. Stuart
1997	Rev. Linda A. Shevlin
1998	Rev. Wee-Li Tan
1999	Rev. Dr. Robert K. Sweet
2000	Rev. Anne Robertson

Introduction

"But they will not ask his (Jesus') help unless they believe in him, and they will not believe in him unless they have heard of him, and they will not hear of him unless they get a preacher."

Romans 10:14

THE MATHEWSON STREET United Methodist Church in Providence, R.I. knew they had a preacher among preachers. When they heard the Rev. Wilbur Ziegler in the pulpit they knew they were hearing the full Gospel: preaching that was evangelical, calling people to a robust faith in God through Jesus Christ; and preaching that was prophetic, calling people to embody in themselves the life and faith of Jesus in matters of justice, peace and compassion.

To honor their pastor, Mathewson Street Church in 1981 established the Wilbur C. Ziegler Award in Preaching. The award is given annually to one preacher nominated by a congregation and selected by a committee of his or her peers in the New England Conference of the United Methodist Church. This peer committee, Church and Society, reviews the extensive supporting material submitted by a church, including written and taped sermons, and selects the preacher to receive the award in a given year. The much anticipated Ziegler Award is presented at the Annual Conference and the recipient preaches at a Conference worship service; and as a guest, preaches on a following fall Sunday at the Mathewson Street Church. The purpose of this award is explained with this inscription:

"The Wilbur C. Ziegler Award in Preaching has been established as a living reminder of Rev. Ziegler's ministry. Because of his compassion and optimism, his ability, his courage and sensitivity, he has truly been good news among us."

As of June 2000, 20 preachers had been acknowledged for their pulpit work in meeting the standards of the award. Sixteen of these preachers agreed to submit representative sermons for this volume. Fortunately, there are sermons by Dr. Ziegler preserved on tapes. Two sermons preached at Trinity United Methodist Church of Springfield, Mass. during his pastorate there (1968 - 1972) were transcribed.

In presenting these written sermons, I have attempted to retain the writing style of each person. Only minor editorial changes have been made in punctuation and sentence structure to enhance (hopefully) the intended meaning. Some preachers included detailed resource data while others made passing reference to their sources. Intentionally, I've permitted broad license here, believing that sermons are not essays or articles, but a different kind of communication altogether. The intention is not to enhance the preacher's scholarly reputation, but to facilitate God's purpose for transformation, renewal and reformation of a people who humbly declare themselves to be God's people, a people who are about the business and mission of bringing scriptural holiness to the social order of the world as John Wesley taught us.

For years I have had people ask me: "How do you decide what to preach about? How do you prepare a sermon?" I'm assuming the question behind the questions is: "What goes into the work of sermon preparation?"

Fair question, especially when it is asked by people who listen regularly to sermons during public worship. So, I asked the Ziegler preachers to tell me, if they were so inclined, how they go about their work. Ten of the 16 preachers responded in some detail. The first chapter is a distillation of their reported processes, procedures and insights regarding sermon preparation, which I hope will interest and inform the reader.

Several of the preachers presented here initially demurred about printing sermons, noting that sermons are public events, verbal vehicles used to present and represent the things of Christ. Preaching, by its very nature, is public and includes an interplay among the Holy Spirit, the preacher and the congregation; it is a part of worship in which music, art, symbols, architecture, physical gestures, voice tone and pattern, spiritual preparation, spiritual readiness and human need all combine for a unique event. The personality of the preacher flavors and seasons the words that are spoken. In many instances a long-established trust between a preacher and her/his congregation freight meanings that are often unspoken, yet powerful in their capacity to transform life.

Rev. David Purdy used an arresting metaphor to talk about sermon writing and delivery: "Sermon writing is an art; preaching an art form. Like an artist with the vision of the completed painting in her mind quickly sketches out the forms and fills in the colors, so sometimes preparing a sermon felt to me to be, literally, an inspired act. ... and God's voice would come through."

This is the art form part of a sermon that cannot, I think, be presented in a book. Moreover, preaching is a unique interaction between preacher and congregation during worship. The art form emerges, I am persuaded, when the preacher permits her/his work in the study to take flesh in public. It is a letting go of possession. "My sermon" becomes "the sermon." God can and will use the bones of the preacher's preparation to support, give form and shape to a living event of a gathered people as they ponder, ingest, refine, or for that matter, reject, the word of the Lord as that word filters through that preacher.

However, having said that sermons are more than literary documents, there is, I am persuaded, still considerable value in engaging the art and reading the word structure of the preacher's thought, insight and faith perspective. In the written form we can see, review, ponder, ingest or reject the thought, insight and faith of the preacher at *a different pace* than in the listening/worship mode. In written form, sermons can and do serve as mentors and accessible guides. We can return again and again. Moreover, the written sermon can be informative for the faith of people yet to come — those who might happen upon this volume to learn and discern some of the faith struggles of the last three decades of the 20th century in New England Methodism.

So, in my mind's eye, I see each sermon in this volume being preached by people who are members of a preaching order, set apart for a special purpose within the United Methodist Church. These preachers, most of whom I know well and hold in the highest regard, have been faithful to the covenant to take the authority given by the church to preach and teach the word of God in Christ for this age and time.

William C. Coleman
Nov. 1, 2000

Some Reflections on Sermon Development

Where do we begin?

Rev. Dr. William C. Coleman

SURELY NO ONE will be surprised that the Ziegler preachers begin with the Bible, the core authoritative text of the Christian faith. Most are also lectionary preachers. They follow suggested readings for given Sundays, providing broad coverage of biblical themes during the year. The readings usually draw from Hebrew Scripture and the New Testament (an epistle and a Gospel lesson), and correspond to the church calendar year and themes. However, the readings are not always integrated around common themes in any discernible way. While there are several lectionaries that circulate within the Christian Church, likely the most commonly used by United Methodists is the Revised Common Lectionary, found in *The United Methodist Book of Worship,* 1992. Often these readings are examined days, sometimes weeks, in advance of a given Sunday, to encourage a filtering, or a percolation process, to happen within the preacher. Thus, themes and insights emerge over time.

Several preachers note that after reading the scriptural texts, they also read commentaries and other resources to enrich and broaden the context of the intellectual/spiritual writing. Rev. Scott Campbell says that he often does his reading without his shoes on, as a symbolic reminder that he is on "holy ground" in this encounter with Scripture.

Rev. David Purdy emphasizes that preaching is done in a community context, and that he is acutely aware—now as a superintendent presiding over more than one congregation—that, as a pastor, his reading of

Scripture is often filtered through an awareness of given pastoral concerns and needs within a congregation. Rev. David Hollenbeck, Rev. David Myers and I have profited from being in ecumenical lectionary study groups. These groups usually meet weekly or monthly to reflect with, and share with, colleagues about interpreting upcoming lectionary readings. For some 12 years, on a weekly time frame, I have feasted gratefully at a shared table with six to 10 area pastors, men and women, who have offered insights and interpretation of Scripture that I dare say would never have occurred to me alone in my study.

Rev. Shirley Hoover and Rev. Frances Swartz, both lectionary preachers, occasionally use a drama/guided imagery in their preaching. Both have representative sermons of this approach. It appears that this preaching model may mirror something of the way they go about their study of the scriptural text. This preaching format encourages the listener to be in the Scripture text itself, blending in one's own personal imagination and experience. In practice, this process very well may also teach a congregation to read Scripture systematically and encourage its reading outside the corporate worship time, as the Scripture becomes accessible in a new, more dramatic way.

The sum and substance is that lectionary study provides preachers with a grounding in the biblical texts themselves, routinely informing preaching, guarding against tunnel vision or relying on favorite preaching texts, and offering a well-balanced scriptural diet to feed the soul. Lectionary study assists a preacher to think biblically and to see the larger, broader themes that thread themselves throughout the Bible, rather than to be myopically centered on a few.

With whom do we dialogue?

Karl Barth is credited with the statement that we ought to have a "Bible in one hand and the newspaper in the other," the point being that each addresses the other. Two of our number specially emphasize how books, periodicals, and newspaper resources, in addition to Scripture, inform them in life-changing ways. All the people whose sermons are included in this volume tell us: read, read, read! Barth, of course, came from a generation which was virtually pre-cinema and pre-television. Were he speaking to us today, it is likely he would add cinema, television and public radio to the linear media. In addition to the printed word, the world of mass media provides a rich insight into modern life and issues. Their influence can hardly be overemphasized. Wisely, Rev. David Hollenbeck has that pen and little notebook ever ready to jot down thoughts about images and dialogue from various media, which are later grist for sermon material. One of Rev. David Purdy's sermons uses a film as a launching pad to help us consider some issues of reconciliation and redemption.

Rev. Anne Robertson and Rev. Rob Stuart lift up in their comments about sermon preparation, two literary resources they have found to have important value: a journal, *The Living Pulpit* and Walter J. Ong's *Orality and Literacy.* Rev. David Hollenbeck may be at the far end of the source spectrum when he acknowledges that he has been known to write a sermon in a truckstop diner. He concludes, "It's a wonderfully real atmosphere."

I have made a point in each church I served to find one or two people who liked to clip or hand me articles they would recommend for my reading. What an invaluable resource those people were to me, affording economy in reading time, yet expanding coverage of material from primary secular sources.

All those who responded to the question regarding sermon preparation and delivery, spoke of the *community context,* or *pastor and people in dialogue.* Rev. David Myers, for example, after nine trips to Nicaragua, found that North American Christian work in that situation was often viewed by some native Nicaraguan Christians in a minimalist, if not disparaging manner as "Good Samaritan" work. He wrote: "I have often been troubled by that phrase, because I have a fundamentally different understanding of the parable. I also wanted to reinforce that mission work is not about doing things for, or to, people of another culture, but rather the notion that we are in mission with them. Indeed, I wanted to share how much la Iglesia de Cristo has changed my faith and life."

Similar *diagnostic activity* was expressed by each of the 10 preachers in their responses to sermon preparation. Parish visitation, casual conversations or remarks as people exit the sanctuary and greet the pastor tell us much, if we listen with a third ear. Rev. David Purdy's sermon *"Go Kiss a Frog"* is a wonderful example of listening with the third ear. He discreetly shares with a congregation, in another place, the dialogue that went on during a terrible crisis in a young woman's life.

Rev. Shirley Hoover's sermon *"On Violence"* reflects a lifetime of listening to, and analyzing, our culture's violence. About this sermon she writes: "I think this is the best sermon I ever preached. I finally got it all together and said effectively what has been on my heart for a very long time. I think the words of my mouth and the meditation of my heart were acceptable in God's sight."

"Today Is Easter," a sermon by Rev. Mark Fowler, focuses on Jesus' resurrection. He grounds God's resurrection event to the life of a congregation which he knows to be grieving and ruminating over the death of a beloved and talented parishioner. Mark notes that the man he cites, Tom, had agreed to have his story told after his death. Mark's handling and interpretation of this story is to be commended, and surely some healing came to that congregation in Needham from interpreting that circumstance.

Dr. Seward Hiltner, who did seminal work in pastoral care education, provides a paradigm that systematically describes the work of dialogue between pastor and congregation, and the diagnostic work that can inform the focus for preaching. In brief, he invites us to identify and name the spirit problems which need addressing, as well as to name and lift up healthy responses which people make to life issues. He urges us to make a conscious commitment to assess the person's or congregation's *personality, situation and spiritual state.* The purpose is not to be clinical, or to pigeonhole, or to label a person or group; rather, it is an attempt to answer the question: What is going on in this person's—or congregation's life?

Practically speaking, this means that the preacher's diagnosis, assessment or analysis, factors in some, if not all, of the following questions:

1. Do the responses reveal the capacity to will, to do, and to make decisions that are consistent with a basic faith perspective within one's religious tradition?
2. Do the responses demonstrate a capacity for gratitude (to receive grace), or for self-forgiveness/forgiveness of others? Or do the responses reveal a kind of narcissism—"I am the ultimate judge

and master of what is right to do and be?"

3. Does the individual or congregation have a clear sense of calling or vocation that comes from beyond one's occupation or livelihood? Can he/she/they own it and act on that call? Does the calling facilitate a sense of responsibility for one's own conduct?
4. Does the faith perspective encourage a person to reach out and care for others, as well as allow one's self to be cared for by others? Or is one's care-giving really a hidden deceptive, self-serving desire to gain acceptance from, or control over, others?
5. What is the awareness of the holy? What is regarded as sacred? What is revered? What is untouchable?
6. Is there a sense of finitude, personal limits? How is ambiguity handled? How is divine purpose regarded? Is there divine help? What help is expected? Who and what are trusted? Who are the wished for saviors?

It is likely that most preachers do, in fact, make assessments of a situation, without formally recognizing or articulating what they are about. Hiltner's model of assessment provides a tool with which to be more intentional, if not systematic and focused, in how we go about our work as doctors of the soul.

Surprisingly, the 10 respondents overtly mentioned nothing about the use of Christian tradition. I suspect this is implied throughout their responses, especially in the use of commentaries and interpretation sources. But let us now make it explicit. Scripture cannot be rightly understood unless there is a thorough, ongoing developmental understanding of the original context and background out of which that text grows. Moreover, familiarity with how the church has, over the years, interpreted given biblical texts, grounds us even closer to the whole Christian community in addition to the contemporary and immediate one. Rev. Robert Sweet brings this point home in his sermon *"Ten Commandments or Ten Suggestions."*

What are we to say and how do we say it?

In some ways the sermons speak for themselves. Yet the process of deciding what to say is not always self-evident. Clearly, each preacher is careful to focus on a central point, a controlling idea or theme. Anne

Robertson puts the goal of the matter succinctly, "No more three points in a sermon and ending with a poem!" For her, ideally, the sermon can be summarized in one sentence, and usually she does not begin to write her sermon until she has that summary sentence on the page.

Rob Stuart reports that he seeks to develop or decide on a metaphor that represents the point(s) he wants to make. He begins by jotting down a variety of points that could be made and then narrows it back again to a main point that may have several sub-points. Sometimes, he uses a complete sermon manuscript and sometimes an outline, but both are pruned several times in order to keep it "simple." He adds a footnote about this: "Keeping it simple refers to the outline, not the content." By wrestling with the meaning of the scriptural text, distilling the ideas that emerge about that text, and reframing the insights that have emerged for current application, "the sermon often gets more profound even as it gets more compelling, more pointed, less filled with distractions and digression."

Whether to use a manuscript, outline or brief notes— about that, there is no consensus. Some of us, Rev. Shirley Hoover and I, for instance, invariably use a full manuscript. Ms. Hoover explains why she opts for using a full manuscript: "I use a manuscript because it prevents me from distracting myself and wandering all over the lot. It is too easy to throw in irrelevant stories or additional material that add nothing to people's understanding of God's word. I'd rather preach a tightly woven sermon that says what it has to say, and stops when it is finished!"

However, at the other end of the spectrum, many of us have marveled for years at Rev. Richard Black's style of sermon development and preaching. He reports going for a walk, thinking through what he wants to say in response to the scriptural texts, jotting down a few notes (probably on the back of a used envelope), and speaking extemporaneously on a given Sunday. In any case, there is no substitute for careful preparation. From all reports it is quite evident that significant groundwork through reading, careful listening, digesting, thinking and reflection goes into Mr. Black's sermon preparation—a process that only appears effortless, like all good art. Yet others report writing out the full text of the sermon, reducing it to an outline, memorizing the main points and then delivering the sermon, either from behind the pulpit or from the center of the chancel. (Like with whether to use a manuscript, outline or brief notes there is no consensus on mode of delivery.)

Perhaps the most central feature of all the sermons in this volume is a weaving together of faith and practice into an integrated whole. Rev. Scott Campbell provides us with two fine examples of storytelling sermons: one about a woman who did not easily fit into a middle class congregation. The other, a response to a letter from a niece, traces how one congregation grew and developed in their perspective toward homosexuals. Such stories can provide a spine on which to bring faith perspectives and a process of faith/response development, in one instance by an individual, and in the other, by a congregation. Rev. Robert Moore's "Love in Living Deeds to Show" masterfully blends his own shared ambivalence and vulnerability with sound scholarship. He invites his congregation to struggle with him in developing faith-filled answers based on the religion of Jesus, to develop their stance toward homosexuality.

Additionally, in all the sermons, congregants are invited to claim faith in Jesus and to embody the faith of Jesus. Six of our preachers provide for us in their sermons what I regard and name as a *teaching, pedagogical style.* The Reverends Landon Lindsay, Richard Black, John Almond, Robert Stuart, Wee-Li Tan and Bob Sweet want us to know something important. They tell us what that is. Then they marshal and lay out the material in a forceful, straightforward manner. They remind us we will be better off if we know what they know, do what they suggest, then do one's best. Their prescription comes close to a comment attributed to Martin Luther, which I will borrow and paraphrase: "Being fallible, let us sin bravely for Jesus."

Of course, we have not mined the full richness of these sermons in these few words, but perhaps this brief introduction will serve as a stimulus for your own examination, appreciation, and learning something about what this company of preachers regards as important to their craft and to faith/practice proclamation. Whatever else these preachers can teach us, they are emphatic about the need for: 1) broad and deep insight into biblical themes and history by systematic Bible reading; 2) paying close attention to the life and agenda of the world; 3) reflective, dialogical thinking and analysis about the implications for the life of faith that the world's agenda presents to us.

To some degree, preachers are like beachcombers, sorting through the flotsam and jetsam of human life, examining and searching for valuables. After carefully reflecting on what is found, then, and only then, under the tutoring of Jesus and the Holy Spirit, the sermon becomes a public offering to a gathered worshipping community. The sermon becomes discernment of what it all means, what we should keep, and what we should do. Christian preachers are called, even mandated, to talk to us about Jesus' unfinished business with us and with the world.

The Greatest Irony of All

John 13:1-17

Rev. T. Landon Lindsay

This sermon was preached on Holy Thursday, 1994 at Faith United Parish, Fitchburg, Massachusetts, while Mr. Lindsay was interim pastor. He notes that this sermon was crafted to avoid a sentimental approach to Holy Thursday and to proclaim the amazing grace of God. For there is a need in all of us to know ourselves as sinners, the Judas in us, and to be open to God's grace, even if we think we are beyond it.

TONIGHT, MORE THAN any other time during the Christian year, we remember Judas, a man of changing moods and conflicting loyalties. We remember him because his story is so intimately associated with Jesus' sharing of the Last Supper with his disciples. Judas brings an aura of tragedy to that seemingly congenial gathering in the upper room. His personality and motives stand in vivid contrast to the motives of Jesus—so much so, in fact, that Judas' treachery casts the meaning of the Lord's Supper in particularly sharp relief.

By the time of the Passover meal, Judas had already decided to betray Jesus. He had met with the chief priests and had been paid 30 pieces of silver by them to betray Jesus. So, there Judas sat with the other disciples in the upper room on the night that would signify the beginning of the end for him as it would for Jesus. At that supper Jesus arose and girded himself with a towel and basin in order to wash the disciples' feet. When you and I are confronted with Jesus' action, is not our tendency to cry out, "No, Jesus! Not Judas, too! Don't wash the feet of the betrayer. He is unworthy of your attention and affection."

But that is the irony of it all. In order to be redemptive, love and kindness must be offered freely to everyone, even to those who place self above it, even to those who betray its trust. The suffering love of God reveals its true character, not only by being willing to endure physical pain, but also by becoming vulnerable to those who would reject it. Humiliation walks hand in hand with crucifixion down the road that leads to redemption.

Here, tonight, the irony becomes most acute. We betray the love by our self-centeredness and by our desire to secure our lives above all things. We so naturally think first about ourselves, about our fulfillment, about our comfort, about our happiness. Then, we're startled and embarrassed as the servant Christ stoops to wash our feet just as he stooped to wash the feet of Judas. There is an irony in our Lord's action that we can never fully understand for we ought to be washing his feet. It's when we realize this, when we embrace rather than reject his suffering love, that transformation comes to our hearts, praise to our lips, even tears to our eyes. Tragically enough, though, this was not the case for Judas. He missed the opportunity to be reconciled to the one he had followed as a disciple. When Jesus spoke the words over the bread, "Take, eat, this is my body," and over the cup, "Drink it all of you," Judas was long gone. The irony is that these words were spoken for him, too! True, he had turned his back on Christ's embodiment of suffering love. But suffering love had not turned its back on him. Judas was running away. He was rebelling against the very love that could heal him, as Scripture calls it, the "love that wilt not let me go." But we flee this love, too, don't we?

We flee it when our work becomes an idol and when our worship becomes an inconvenience. We flee it when our fantasies of the good life occupy more of our time than our practice of the disciplined life. We flee it when our striving to obtain our "piece of the rock" consumes us and our scheming "to arrive" absorbs us. Still, all the while, bread is being broken and the cup is being shared in the upper room to dramatize the greatest irony of all—the irony that the further we try to flee from God, the more determined God is to draw near to us.

Yes, Judas, this meal was for you, too! The problem is that you didn't realize it. You were too much at war with yourself to be at peace with

Christ or with the other disciples.

Yet we are all ruined sinners, too! In God's eyes none of us is any better or any worse than Judas Iscariot. But a special opportunity presents itself to us tonight. We can choose once again to be followers of Christ and join him in fellowship at his table. The bread and the cup at this table remind us that even though we might do the worst to God, God does the best for us. There is no depth too deep, no separation too wide, and no time too long to cause God to forget us.

Christ's body was broken and his blood was shed that we might be here tonight, not as God's enemies, but as God's friends, and sisters and brothers to each other. In this there is no irony, only mercy and blessing! Here at his table, Jesus comes to us again, not in body, but in soul and heart. He comes to us in our morning light, our noonday praise and evening joy. He comes to remind us that his brokenness is the means by which we can be made whole and that by his stripes we are healed. Here he prepares a place for us that we can call our own forever. Here he accepts us and promises to treat us as his own dear children, as people who will never be turned away, who will never be left alone, who will never be treated with anything but respect and kindness.

As we come to this supper tonight, we respond to the call that somehow Judas could not, or would not hear—the call to come back to the upper room that we might share a meal with Jesus, and in doing so, find peace and salvation.

How to Receive a New Pastor

I Corinthians 3:5-17

Rev. T. Landon Lindsay

The substance of this sermon has been preached in 1981, 1990 and 1994. Its purpose is twofold: First, to help a congregation receive a new pastor without carrying a lot of unnecessary psychological baggage over into the new relationship. Second, to stimulate the congregation to reflect on their important role in welcoming the new pastor, to help him or her build on existing strengths of the congregation and begin to develop new ministries for the future. This version was preached at Faith United Parish, Fitchburg, Mass. in 1994.

JOHN HUGHES, AN English psychologist, says most of us have very predictable patterns of entering into and exiting from relationships with other people. I quote: "In fact, I believe it goes even deeper. I contend that saying 'hello' and saying 'goodbye' are the two major learning tasks all humans need to accomplish. I would venture that 98 percent of all the people in institutions for the emotionally disturbed are there because they fouled up at either saying 'hello' or saying 'goodbye.' ... Some children come into the world and have no one in the family to say 'hello' to them. Can you imagine what it's like trying to learn to say 'hello' to others in the world, when no one ever said 'hello' to you when you were born."

February 18 - "Hello, Joan." "Goodbye, Landon." We learn about ourselves in how we say "hello" and "goodbye."

How are we to receive a new pastor? Well, first, we say goodbye to the pastor who is leaving. We need to do some grief work! Grief in losing a pastor or an interim, if not expressed, will be carried over into the new relationship. If carried over, the new pastor has to listen to endless stories of a former pastor for a year or so. Inadequately saying goodbye can render us incapable of accepting a new pastor's leadership—for a year or more. Moreover, letting go of old grudges and starting with a clean plate are important for us, people and pastor, so as not to carry unresolved feelings into the new relationship. Hanging onto old hurts leaves no energy for new life. We need to emerge as whole persons. So, it might be helpful, when a new pastor is coming, to write out your feelings and share them with a trusted friend in the church, one who can keep a confidence.

Second, we need to remember that our roles change. My relationship to you as pastor or interim pastor and your relationship to me as a parishioner ends as of Feb. 18th. We enter a new relationship—being friends to each other. A new pastor will do the liturgical and pastoral care work. Certainly, I will need your prayers and support in moving to this new relationship. And I will give you my support and offer prayer for you, not as a pastor, but as a friend. All of us will need to give special effort to accept and honor this new relationship. The Alban Institute, in studying military chaplains, discovered that chaplains accepted the fact that the future ministry of their situation will belong eventually to someone else. Hence, they worked out their goodbyes the most effectively of all clergy.

Sometimes we clergy have more difficulty letting go of the role we played with people than we do letting go of the people themselves. My dying to this parish involves dying to my role with you as well. To hang on would be a bid for immortality! We clergy can allow ourselves to be indispensable with people (at least think we are) in an attempt to live forever in their lives. So, we pastors and people need to see the foolishness of this, and to let go of one another. Now, you have been great and loving to my wife and me. We appreciate that. But now is the time for me to say, "thank you," and to let you go.

It is my policy not to return to a parish I have served for one year. My own integrity requires this and I have talked to Joan, your new pastor, about it. She appreciates this decision very much, though she graciously said that I would be welcome any time.

The third thing I want to lift up about receiving a new pastor is this: Make every effort to understand your new pastor. Remember that a new pastor comes basically as a stranger to most of you. She will have very few friends here, yet. You have been in this parish and you have each other. She has no one, virtually.

"Walk two moons in their moccasins"— so goes the Native American folklore regarding the stranger. Moreover, don't play games with your new pastor. That is, don't sit back and say to yourself, "I'll see if her ideas agree with mine," or, "I'll see if she remembers my name," or "I'll sit back and wait for her to fix everything." Sometimes a congregation expects a messiah to jump-start a church right away, or at least, very soon. The fact is, you have called a pastor with energy and faith. Restarting a church takes energy and faith in God's power in order to ward off discouragement. But one of the common elements in a restart is the pastor's fatigue. If you expect her to fix everything and if she tries to carry through on that expectation, she will burn out.

There are some concrete things you can do to welcome her and to let her know you are with her in revitalizing your church. Let her know in word and deed that you care for and about her. Some suggestions: Write her a welcome note. Encourage others in the parish to be present the very first Sunday she is here. This sanctuary ought to be jammed full! When she arrives, ask her, "What can I do to help you most right now?" When or if differences arise between you and her, remain open to work through any of those differences. Refuse to participate in gossip. Discourage it. Have a wish list for your new pastor. Love your new pastor. Just give love, no strings attached.

Conclusion: Death is the "final stage of growth." In death and grief we do not so much need protection from painful experience, as we need boldness to face it. If we choose love, we must also have the courage to grieve. As painful as termination and the resulting grief might be, we do need to say, "goodbye," before we can really ever say, "hello," to a new relationship. Christians know about this: death before resurrection. Throughout this entire process our faith gets a real work out. We are really best able to lean into the death experience or termination when we live in grace. At some point in this process, we really need to let go and allow God's grace to carry us through the moment. It is just possible that God has a gift for South Church, if we will only loosen our grip on what we've got and open our hand to receive it. This is my prayer, my hope for South Church, as you receive a new pastor.

My Beloved Daughter

Matthew 3:13-17

Rev. William M. "Scott" Campbell

This sermon was preached at Harvard Epworth Church, Cambridge, Mass., Jan. 10, 1999.

IT'S THE VOICE that troubles me ... not that Jesus hears it, but rather, what does it mean? Is it intended to set Jesus apart from us as utterly unique? Certainly, that seems to be Matthew's intent. Yet, I cannot help wondering whether it might mean something else as well. Could it be that this voice from on high declares not only what is true for Jesus, but also what is universally true when repentant people offer themselves to God?

Carolyn lived in a little three-room shack near the banks of the Merrimac River in Salisbury, Mass. She lived there with her grown son, Richard. I never heard anyone mention anything about a husband, and Carolyn never volunteered any information on the subject. Carolyn had a moderate mental disability. She lived on public assistance and whatever Richard could pick up from odd jobs.

There are two other things that you should know about Carolyn. The first is that she was a rather large woman who did not exercise very careful personal hygiene. There was always a rather overwhelming combination of body odor and powder about her. The second thing that you have to know about Carolyn is that she loved to come to church.

I don't remember how I first met her, but I know that it wasn't very long before I was making regular Sunday morning runs from Newburyport over to Salisbury to pick her up before church. She didn't have a car and no one else in the church was willing to go. I was young and idealistic and believed that anyone who wanted to come to church ought to be able to come, even those who didn't smell very good, and even if the pastor had to pick him or her up.

The phone calls started the next day. By Saturday I was informed that no one could make Tuesday's Bible study and that I ought to consider canceling for this week. I was incensed. For the very first time in my ministry, I prepared a "Thus saith the Lord" sermon. I preached with the passion that only a seminarian with a first cause could muster. The only thing that restrained me at all was the need to be somewhat circumspect because Carolyn was sitting in the congregation. As far as I know, she never caught onto what was happening.

That Tuesday every one of the Bible study members showed up at Carolyn's. (That was when I first learned the short-term motivating power of pure, unadulterated guilt!) I'm happy to report that we all survived and Carolyn was the almost perfect hostess. The only minor glitch came when she served the coffee. For most of us, it was our first introduction to what Carolyn described as "the old Yankee custom" of putting salt in the coffee instead of sugar. There are some traditions that ought not to be perpetuated!

I left the Newburyport Church in the spring of 1974 and willed Carolyn to my successor, Alan Anderson. I didn't hear from her for about a year and a half. Then one fine October day, the phone rang. It was Carolyn. "I'm calling to ask you the biggest favor I ever asked a preacher," she said.

I could feel my stomach tightening. "What could that be, Carolyn?"

"I've made a decision that I want to be baptized. I don't know how much longer I've got to live especially since I can't seem to quit these darn cigarettes. So, this is the time and I want you and Alan to baptize me next Saturday."

Relieved now, I told her that as long as it was OK with Alan, I would be pleased to participate, but I wondered why she wanted it on a Saturday.

"There's one part I didn't tell you about yet," she added.

The knot came back to my stomach. "What didn't you tell me, Carolyn?"

"I want to have it done in the Seabrook River. My friend got baptized there last summer and it was really something special."

"But Carolyn, it's not summer anymore. This is October. Do you have any idea how cold that water is going to be?"

"The weatherman says it's supposed to be sunny and warm this weekend," she countered.

OK. Normally I would push for a baptism to happen in church, but Carolyn clearly had chosen a setting that was meaningful to her, and besides, technically, I was just there to help Alan. I agreed to be there at two o'clock the next Saturday afternoon.

Carolyn had planned everything. She had invited her cousin and her cousin's husband to be witnesses. My wife also came along to round out the congregation. She was even right about the weather. It wasn't such a bad October afternoon. The only thing that she had forgotten to take into account was that the Seabrook River is a tidal river and low tide that day occurred at precisely 1:56 p.m. We had to walk about a hundred yards through shin deep mud to even get close to any water. Carolyn had insisted on wearing loafers, which were both lost within the first 10 steps.

By the time we got out to waist deep water, the little band of witnesses on the distant shore was fading from view. Alan and I weren't exactly sure how to proceed. We were Methodists, after all, not Baptists. We began with prayer, followed by the examination of the candidate.

"Do you truly and earnestly repent of your sins and accept Jesus Christ as your savior?" I asked.

"I do," Carolyn replied.

"Do you believe in God the Father almighty, maker of heaven and earth; and in Jesus Christ his only son our Lord; and in the Holy Spirit, the Lord, the giver of life?" Alan questioned her.

"Yes, I do," she responded.

Together, one on either side of her, we laid her back into the cold salt water. "We baptize you in the name of the Father, and of the Son, and of the Holy Spirit," we declared in unison. Carolyn was startled by the frigid water coming over her face and had a moment of panic. She began kicking her feet. We struggled to lift her out of the water. I mentioned, didn't I, that she was a very large woman? It was anything but graceful, but we did manage to get her up. The water ran down over her round face. She was coughing and smiling. One of us spoke a benediction and she laughed all the way through it. The baptism was finished. We trudged back to the beach through the mud. Carolyn wanted everyone to come back to her house for a party. How could we not rejoice with her.

Carolyn, who had never really fit in at her church, who could not seem to master the ways of polite society, who put others off by her unappealing ways, had, at long last, found her way home. In her baptism she was no misfit. In baptism she stood on equal footing with all of the saints and apostles; she was one with kings and queens, popes and paupers alike; in her baptism she was united with Christ. She belonged as you belong and as I belong. At last.

When I think back on it, when I remember struggling to lift her from the water, and I recall looking into her coughing, smiling, laughing face, would you think it strange if I told you that in the silence of memory I, too, can hear a voice whispering? The words are hard to distinguish, but I think I know what they are saying. I think the voice is telling anyone who will hear, "This is my beloved daughter. With her, I am well pleased."

Carolyn was right about the cigarettes. She died of a heart attack about a year after the October baptism. I don't think of her often these days, but she always comes to mind when I read about the baptism of Jesus. But do you know the strangest thing of all? For all these years, I've had something backwards. All the time I thought that I was the one reaching out to her. It is only now that I understand that she was the one with a mission. Though she never would have spoken in such terms, I can see now that she was an instrument of God, used to teach a young preacher something about the mind-boggling inclusiveness of God's family, and to remind this well-into-middle-aged preacher how easy it is to forget that simple lesson. Amen.

When Silence Isn't Enough

Luke 4:16-21

Rev. William M. "Scott" Campbell

This sermon was preached at Harvard Epworth Church, Cambridge, Mass., May 16, 1999.

I RECEIVED AN E-MAIL on Friday of this week from my college-age niece. She was writing to alert me to a "five-minute opportunity (I had) to witness for Christ." According to her letter, the Anheuser Busch Brewery is test-marketing a commercial showing two gay men drinking a beer together. Fearing an overwhelming negative response, the e-mail continued, the company has set up a hot line for people to register their disapproval. My niece invited me to take a Christian stand by calling the number, and further urged me to encourage my congregation to send a strong message to this company that Christians would not tolerate this assault on our values.

I had a dilemma. What should I do about her letter? I obviously wasn't going to do what she wanted me to do, but how should I handle her? She is a wonderful young woman who has grown up in a highly conservative environment. To my way of thinking, her letter came more out of ignorance than malice, but what should I do? Should I take on the whole question via e-mail? Should I write a clever note back asking whether I was supposed to protest their sexual orientation or their choice of beverage?

I hate to tell you this, but my first temptation was to ignore the whole business. Unfortunately, I had already decided by that point in the week that I was going to preach on the topic, "When Silence Isn't Enough"; even the bulletin was already printed! It was too late to change my mind.

This, friends, was proof to me, if proof was ever needed, that God has a wonderful sense of humor.

And so, with great reluctance, because speaking the truth, as we know it, to those we love is the hardest kind of witnessing we can do, I decided not to remain silent and to write her the following letter:

> My Dearest Niece,
>
> I received your e-mail the other day. It was ironic that it came two days before our congregation was to gather to celebrate an important decision it made several months ago. On second thought, maybe it wasn't ironic—perhaps it was the Holy Spirit at work.
>
> In any case, let me tell you about what we decided and why and how all this relates to your letter. After a process of study and prayer over a period of 18 months, our congregation came to understand that we in the church have sinned against a group of people in our world. The strange thing is that this is not a group of strangers or a distant enemy. On the contrary, they are our own brothers and sisters, sons and daughters, mothers and fathers. I am speaking, of course, about the gay and lesbian and bisexual people who live their lives in the midst of our lives.
>
> During the course of our study, we came to understand that the church has often sent a message to such people that made them feel unwelcome and unwanted. We further came to believe that the predominant message of Jesus Christ was a message of inclusion and acceptance. The only way that our congregation could put these two lessons learned together was to declare that we would not rest comfortably with things as they were; we would seek to heal the wounds that Christians have too often inflicted on other children of God. We declared ourselves to be a "Reconciling Congregation," a church that is "truly open to all people," regardless of their sexual orientation.

The Gospel lesson at our church for this Sunday is taken from Luke 4. Jesus declares that he has come "to proclaim release to the captives, and recovery of sight to the blind, to set at liberty those who are oppressed." This quotation from Isaiah is the text Jesus chooses to begin his ministry. It is no small thing in his mind. In fact, for the rest of his life he is in trouble with the religious authorities of his day because he includes people they consider unclean and sinful in his company. He eats and drinks with them and talks with them and heals their diseases by laying his hands on them.

There are lots of things we could discuss, many of which would make for interesting debate. We could talk about what we ought to make of the prohibitions against homosexual acts in the Bible or, for that matter, the biblical acceptance of prostitution, slavery and polygamy. Or we could debate whether we believe one's sexual identity is chosen or God-given. We could tell stories about homosexual people we have known who have suffered outrageously or who, themselves, have transgressed against the community. All this discussion, I'm sure, would be interesting and important, especially if we were able to listen to each other with open minds and open hearts. But for me, right now, none of those topics are nearly as important as my fundamental conviction about what is at the heart of the Gospel—namely, the inclusive, embracing love of Jesus Christ.

It is no accident that Matthew's story of final judgment asks not a single doctrinal question. There is no discussion before the throne of God about who observed the law or who didn't, or who followed the rules and who didn't. The only concerns of Christ are: Who had a compassionate heart? Who fed the hungry and welcomed the stranger? Who clothed the naked and visited the sick and those in prison? Those are the questions for which we are ultimately accountable.

> Our church decided that no matter what we believe personally about human sexuality, the greatest sin we could commit would be to attempt to close the doors of the church to anyone. Those doors do not belong to us, but to Jesus. How could we exclude anyone in his name?
>
> Please understand, I know it would not be your intention to exclude people. I know your heart is way too big for that, but I think it is important that you recognize that when you participate in a campaign which identifies certain people as beyond the bounds of acceptability, not for what they have done, but for who they are, you are joining in an action which is terribly hurtful to people Jesus loves. It is also important to recognize that all Christian people do not agree with the stands that many in the church have taken against these sisters and brothers, and that none of us, on either side of the debate, can claim to have the Christian position on this issue.
>
> I want to close this letter by telling you how proud I am of you. I believe that the ministry you have been engaged in during your time in the Northwest is a wonderful indication of the grace that is in you. I have written this letter to you not to condemn you, but to share a perspective with you that Christian people in another part of the country have arrived at in good faith, out of their own deep struggle to understand the word that God is speaking in our day.
>
> Much love,
>
> Your Uncle Scott

So there it is. I don't know what will come of it, but I will send it tonight, trusting that as inadequate as my words might be, silence would simply not suffice.

Weeping with Rachel

Isaiah 63:7-9; Hebrews 2:10-18; Matthew 2:13-18

Rev. Richard E. Black

This sermon was preached at St. Matthew's United Methodist Church, Acton, Mass. during Rev. Mr. Black's appointment as pastor.

ISN'T IT STRANGE that, having just celebrated the birth of Jesus and the coming of the Wise Men, the topic suddenly seems to shift to suffering? In the reading from Isaiah we hear of the suffering of the people and of God being at one with them. In the reading from Hebrews we hear the same, that the savior having come into the world chooses to identify with the poor and broken, and to give up his life for their redemption. So it is with the Gospel reading.

However, we may have heard this story so often that we fail to recognize the dimensions of the horrible tragedy it depicts. Can you imagine the scene? Soldiers entering the small villages around Bethlehem kicking down doors, looking for children two years old and younger and when finding them, killing them right in front of their parents. Can you imagine what it must have been like to be a parent trying to hide your children, fleeing your house, looking for cover behind even a small bush, or a grain pile muffling the sobs of your baby only to be discovered and have the child hacked to death before your eyes? How unbelievably horrible this scene is, and it comes to us right at Christmastide which is our time of family celebration. The season of peace and good will is suddenly confronted by this tragedy.

What can Matthew be telling us by the placement of this story? By placing these stories of the Wise Men and Herod's revenge so close together, one might think Matthew is placing two opposites, joy and sorrow, in juxtaposition to remind us that both are part of life. That is a true and powerful message, but I think there is something else at work here. Joy and sorrow are both expressions of passion and as such are related. The tragedy in this story stems not from the passion which we encounter, but from the apathy of Herod, his inability to feel at all. Joy and sorrow are related because they both touch us at the deepest level of our being. They open us to the passion of life. I suspect that this is what Matthew may be trying to do for us. He places the joyous story of the Wise Men finding Jesus in the manger and presenting their gifts just before this horrible scene of children being ruthlessly murdered by this maniacal king. Joy and sorrow, the capacity to experience the fullness of life, emerge from the same wellspring which is passion.

One of the greatest gifts that God gives us through the incarnation is the capacity to live passionately. When we live passionately, we are able to lose ourselves in the moment and to live from the soul. It is in living from the soul that we are able to experience joy and sorrow, and we discover that all of us in our common humanity are bound together. We are bound more tightly by that than we are separated by all the difference of our colors, sizes, shapes, national origins, politics and whatever else we would use to separate ourselves from one another. The unifying elements of the human experience spring from that passion for life. Perhaps Herod recognized this and, perhaps, it was that which so frightened him about this baby. He knew that if this Jesus unlocked a passion for life in the people and they experienced their common humanity, then they would no longer tolerate his cruel, unjust, vicious rule.

Walter Brueggeman in his wonderful little book, *The Prophetic Imagination,* talks about passion for life being the fundamental message of the prophets and Jesus. He goes on to say that when we can feel passion for life, then the seeds of the reign of God are sown in us—for it is in passion that we begin to take each other seriously. It is in passion that we begin to see life in all its immense possibilities. It is in passion that we learn to love.

Love and passion are dangerous for those who would deny humanity its freedom, its dignity, its justice. No wonder Herod was afraid. He was a man filled with the fear of losing his power and this rendered him unable to feel the passion of others. Unable to feel compassion, he was disconnected from humanity, and in his apathy he could murder infants.

This apathy, this disconnect we encounter in Herod, is an issue in our culture and in our time. We are easily mesmerized and rendered insensitive to humanity around us. Whether we recognize the reality or not, we are the powerful in the world and we have much to lose if passion is unleashed. We very often let ourselves hide behind a wall of apathy and pretend that what is so, is so because we deserve to be wealthy and powerful. How often do we feel righteous indignation, tragedy and pain, wonder and joy? Where is the passion, the joy, yes, the hearty laughter? We are diminished in our daily lives to watching reruns of "I Love Lucy" rather than engage in conversations which touch the soul. We forget how to laugh with gusto and spirit, but instead allow television producers to put a laugh track on their shows to tell us when to laugh? Or, we use a chemical. We have come to a point in our culture where we are so dulled that we cannot feel the joy which springs from deep within us, the passion for life.

The same is true for the tragedies of life. We can look at a world where people cannot find work, who cannot find jobs, who cannot support their families, and we reduce the suffering to a set of numbers called the "jobless rate." There are people who sleep each night in doorways or on subway grates and we reduce that sad state to the "homeless rate." When there are battles and wars, we find a way to trivialize the suffering by keeping score with body counts. And the winner today is whoever got the most opponent bodies in plastic bags to be shipped home to grieving parents and families. Numbers and figures.

I was in Guatemala during the insurgency, when the army passed through villages of indigenous people suspected of harboring subversives. In the villages, the army mimicked the actions of Herod's soldiers. Pregnant women were dissected, babies smashed against walls, men tortured and disemboweled. All of this was done against the poor in the name of a political ideology. Where was our complaint? We have become desensitized to both the joys and tragedies of life. What has happened to our passion? Where is our ability to feel, to laugh, to hug, to dance, to cry? Have we become like Herod? Are we so tied to what we own and our status in life that we will build a wall of apathy in order to keep it?

The gift that Matthew holds out for us at Christmas is revealed in two stories set side by side. One, which moves us to a sense of profound joy, is the story of the three kings who would sacrifice everything to travel hundreds of miles to kneel at the feet of this unlikely child called Jesus. They laugh and hug and give their wealth to this child and in doing so, they know the profound sense of being fulfilled in his presence. Their lives have taken on new meaning and they are connected to the fullness of what it is to be alive. They live with passion. Right next to that, Matthew sets the horrible story of a king so vicious and vile that he would murder even babies to preserve his rule. He tells us of Rachel weeping, of all the mothers of Bethlehem in tears. He tells us of suffering so profound as to be beyond words. He tells us of a king so apathetic that he can no longer sense the tragic dimension of what he has done. And, he tells us of Jesus, who is present at the moment of laughter and present at the moment of tears. He tells us of Jesus who through the incarnation can open the Wise Men to a joy and fulfillment so profound that it is beyond words. He tells us of Jesus present in the moment of tragedy who weeps with Rachael and her daughters and comforts them in their grief. He tells us of Herod who is so lost in his own fears that he can no longer experience either joy or grief and who has lost the ability to have compassion. And finally, he offers us a choice.

Shall we live inside the shell of apathy which the rich and powerful build around themselves and which becomes their prison, or shall we live to the depths and the height of life? Shall we drink deeply from the cup of the soul and be liberated to incarnate the spirit within us? This is the gift of this season, to unlock within us and to break down around us the wall that prevents us from living life in all its passion. In so doing, we sow the seeds of the reign of God. May God help us in the name of this child, Jesus, to unlock the passion in our own souls that we may laugh and cry, sing and dance, and hold one another in our arms and hearts, grieve and comfort, be alive. Amen.

Authentic Leadership

Rev. Richard E. Black

No scriptural text was cited as this was a sermon prepared and preached in 1999 for a group of business leaders who are interested in spiritual formation. The Rev. Mr. Black is appointed to "extension ministries" and is employed as a consultant to business and industry.

SHORTLY AFTER HIS release from a quarter of a century in prison, often in solitary confinement, Nelson Mandela traveled to the United States on a triumphant tour. Huge crowds in every city in which he appeared greeted him as a hero. Here was a man who would not be broken, who would not dwell in bitterness, who never wavered from a vision so powerful that it had transformed even his jailers. When Mandela came to Boston, my daughter and I were part of a crowd of thousands that began to gather well before his scheduled appearance on the Esplanade next to the Charles River, excitedly waiting for a glimpse of and a word from this extraordinary man. The crowd, which included black and white, old and young, men and women, rich and poor, transcended our usual self-imposed homogeneous boundaries. It was humanity gathered!

There is a charisma in the leadership of Nelson Mandela, which transcends race, culture and religion. There is something in his leadership which speaks to the human spirit, to that which is most personal and profound, yet most universal and shared. He speaks to common human yearnings which, when articulated, seem self-evident and obvious.

Nelson Mandela's leadership has historical precedents; it is not unique. Other leaders have had such power. Mohandas Gandhi liberated India from the mighty British Empire and even confounded Winston

Churchill. Martin Luther King Jr. spoke to the higher angels of the human spirit when he galvanized the American civil rights movement. Marion Wright Edelman has made the cause of defending children a crusade that has enrolled thousands. Millard Fuller's dream of "no more shacks" has brought millions into the Habitat for Humanity organization. The list of such leaders stretches back to great religious figures like Moses, Jesus, Buddha and a host of others that epitomize this galvanizing, energizing and transforming leadership. Such leaders can also be found in the world of business. Tom Chapell and his company, *Tom's of Maine,* with its commitment to a humane workplace and environmentally friendly products, are an example. So is Ray Anderson's commitment to a livable planet which has transformed his company, *Interface, Inc.* What can we learn from such leaders? How can what they intuitively know and demonstrate enable today's leaders to be more effective and find deeper satisfaction in what they do?

There is something in the leadership of Mandela and those we have mentioned which we shall call "authentic." When we use the term "authentic leadership," we do not mean real leadership, or right leadership, or the only leadership. In using the term authentic, we are trying to point to a kind of leadership which derives from a profound source which unifies mind (rational/conceptual), body (physical/senses), and spirit (soul), which the leader has integrated in his/her life.

The action that an authentic leader takes is consistent with his/her most deeply held convictions and beliefs, which derive from this source and which are referred to in a number of ways. Physicist David Bohm speaks of the "implicate order." Theologian Paul Tillich referred to "the ground of being." The Jewish biblical tradition calls it "wisdom" while in the Christian tradition, St. John calls it "logos." Some call it spirit, others soul. In using the term authentic leadership, we are denoting a kind of leadership which manifests the foundational element of all being, and which is fundamental to our biblical understanding of the world.

Thus, the authentic leader has wisdom. Wisdom, as understood in the biblical tradition, is far different than our contemporary understanding of that word. In the biblical tradition, wisdom is the source of all that exists. It is the framework, the principle, the truth, the harmony, which God uses in fashioning something out of nothing and which keeps all of creation in a state of shalom, peace or order and keeps it from spinning into disconnected fragments. Wisdom is not a set of rules. It cannot be owned nor fully mastered but only accessed, and the point of access is the soul. Wisdom infuses all that is, so the mind can glimpse it and the body can experience it, but neither can encompass it. Wisdom is not the accumulation of information, but it is enlightenment. It is connected to the logos, which is universal and foundational and which unifies all of reality.

A distinction between reason and wisdom is crucial. Reason is a tool that analyzes to find the answer by dividing reality into parts and trying to understand each part. Wisdom uses reason and adds to it the sense of wholeness that binds all of reality together. By its nature, wisdom unifies and integrates. Without reason, wisdom can be an ethereal spirituality anchored in nothing. Without wisdom, reason can be a valueless tool.

What does any of this have to do with leadership in our time? It is wisdom that Nelson Mandela has accessed as the source of his remarkable power. By living out of this wisdom, he and other remarkable leaders like him communicate on a level that enables them to transcend artificial boundaries and integrate people and ideas in creative ways. This ability to integrate enables them to envision possibilities which are far more compelling than those drawn from a fragmented worldview. This creates an effortless flow of energy which gives their lives the unmistakable stamp of authenticity.

A definition for authentic leadership is elusive. It is a bit like the "I know it when I see it" description, and this is, in fact, one of the characteristics of authentic leadership. We do know it when we see it, because it springs from that place within the leader which is most profound, most powerful, most personal, and yet most universal. We recognize authenticity when we see it because it speaks a language that the soul can comprehend. Authentic leadership is powerful and some of those who have exhibited it have literally shaken the world. There are three critical characteristics which authentic leaders share:

- A clear intention and focus which when articulated is unmistakable, transcendent, and compelling.
- An ability to live in paradox and ambiguity which integrates seemingly disconnected ideas and possibilities.

- An ability to draw out the full potential from others.

Clarity of Intention

An authentic leader has taken the inward journey, opening his/her own soul, and is able to articulate what s/he has discovered as most important for her/his life. This creates a clarity of vision in which goals become simpler and yet more profound. They derive from the integration of what were, heretofore, fragmented strands of life. While the result is a sharper focus, the focus does not narrow, but broadens the horizon of possibilities. A sense of purpose and urgency emerges. The soul is the source of the vision and the vision, when shared, enrolls others, enabling them to free their souls, for it comes from that place which is common to all humans. This clarity of vision and passion for achieving goals invites others to join in a common journey.

When a vision comes from the deepest recesses of the soul, others recognize it as an invitation to join a journey toward something worthwhile. Nelson Mandela had a vision of human liberation transcending race. He articulated that vision in a way that touched the souls of others, and because of this he played the key role in transforming his nation. This commitment based upon a vision of what is possible has a simplicity and clarity that enable it to communicate across class, race and culture. Millard Fuller's vision and commitment is as simple as "no more shacks." Behind this is the full weight of a set of values about human dignity that speaks a universal language. When Martin Luther King Jr. articulated a vision of equality, it was so clear that one could literally see it and even the smallest child could understand. It would be difficult to overestimate the power of a profound vision clearly articulated and visibly lived. In our own cynical age when leaders are not trusted, when spin counts more than truth, and sizzle sells more than steak, such a deep-rooted integrity creates trust and eagerness to follow.

Living in Ambiguity

Another mark of authentic leadership is the ability to live in ambiguity by holding both sides of a paradox in creative tension. Our training teaches us to seek definitive answers. We do not leave room for ambiguity nor for competing truths to be held simultaneously. In my consulting work, I have encountered many leaders who are searching for silver bullets. They latch on to TQM (Total Quality Movement), Reengineering the Corporation, integrated software packages, innovations in technology, and the list could go on. All of this is in search of the one answer that will put them at the head of the pack. In fact, there is no single answer. Our world is too complex for that.

When we begin to explore the realm of spirit we begin to uncover ambiguity. Singular, definitive answers to fundamental questions are insufficient. Broad principles or understandings that are often intuited rather than rigorously defined replace them. Statements that would seem to be mutually exclusive are equally applicable and can be held simultaneously. Life is no longer colored in stark blacks and whites, but takes on a variety of hues of gray as well. Though living with such ambiguity can at first be disquieting, when we continue to live on this ground, new possibilities open as new contexts and frames of reference emerge. Ray Anderson is simultaneously committed to maximum profitability and zero pollution. This paradoxical commitment has led to significant breakthroughs in how people think at Hiline and what they hold as fundamental values. Mandela's total commitment to black liberation while embracing his white captors led to the transformation even of his white jailers' lives. The tension which emerges when one is willing to live into paradox is the source of creative energy which can make old things new. Jesus' use of parable and story, which allows the listener to find him/herself in the narrative and then make choices, is a reminder of the power of paradox. Jesus does not direct the listener, but allows him/her to choose where to stand. This integrates rather than separates. This creates new possibilities which far outstrip the old.

Unlock Full Potential

It has become axiomatic that most of us only employ a small percentage of our potential. Only a fraction of our brain is actively engaged and we often seem to perform on autopilot when the tasks are repetitious or non-challenging. If we make the presumption that as human beings we are more than physical bodies and more than mental activity, then work that does not engage us at a deeper level can never hope to unleash more than this small portion of our potential abilities.

We often assume that the soulful part of our lives, the most private and personal, should be protected or hidden and has no place in the work environment. A result is, we fragment our lives and feel unfulfilled in the work we do. It is unfortunately true that for many of us the work we perform to earn our living does not call forth the spirit or soul where our most cherished values reside. The authentic leader can open this level and invite participation from this place.

People are desperately seeking a purpose to work for and to live for. When they find it, they invest themselves. The vast reservoir of potential is tapped and the impossible becomes possible. What difference would it make if you were able to unlock the full potential of everyone in your organization and challenge them to attain something remarkable, something really worth doing, something that engaged their whole being?

Conclusion

Today, we are more in need of authentic leaders than ever before. In a global knowledge-based economy with a highly educated work force, managing by the numbers is not sufficient. As Albert Einstein once wrote, "Not everything that counts can be counted, and not everything that can be counted counts." In a rapidly changing global marketplace where agility is required, managing by the rules is insufficient. People want a purpose to work for. They want principles to work by. They want power to get the job done. Authentic leadership taps into that most powerful human resource which is the soul and liberates it for the work to be done. In his inaugural address, Nelson Mandela used the following quote to set the course for his new South Africa:

> Our deepest fear is not that we are inadequate.
> Our deepest fear is that we are powerful beyond measure.
> It is our light, not our darkness that most frightens us.
> We ask ourselves, who are we to be brilliant, gorgeous,
> talented and fabulous?
> Actually, who are you not to be? You are a child of God.
> Your playing small doesn't serve the world
> There is nothing enlightening about shrinking so
> That others will not feel insecure around you.
> We were born to manifest the glory of God within us.

It is not just in some of us, it is in everyone.

And, when we let our own light shine, we unconsciously give others the permission to do the same.
As we are liberated from our own fear, our presence automatically liberates others.

Authentic leadership is about this liberation which unleashes the power of the human spirit in the world, and brings us into Shalom with the world and with one another.

Christians and Gambling

I Timothy 6:6-21

Rev. Frances P. Swartz

This sermon was preached at Central United Methodist Church, Brockton, Mass., Sept. 27, 1998.

ONE OF OUR former presidents, Calvin Coolidge, was well known as being a man of few words. It is said that one Sunday, after he came home from church, someone asked him, "What did the minister preach about?"

"Sin," was the answer.

"Well, what did he say about it?" the questioner persisted

"He's agin' it," replied Coolidge.

I suspect that you already know where I'm going to come down on a sermon about "Christians and Gambling." It's no mystery to you. I am a United Methodist minister after all. And, we have talked and joked about this. "Can't we have a raffle?" someone will say, full well knowing, and accepting, the answer. I have been impressed with your commitment. But I hope that we can say more than what President Coolidge chose to say; I hope that we can talk about why we are "agin it."

Gambling has become more and more pervasive in our country. In 1963, New Hampshire organized a state-sponsored lottery. By the 1970s two dozen states were working on having lotteries. By 1983, gambling was one of the largest leisure industries, to the tune of $135 billion. By 1993, 10 years later, it has grown to $394 billion.

Why should we Christians be concerned about this? In a nutshell, the gambling philosophy runs counter to faith in God. Gambling in fact leads us away from God. Rather than trusting in God, gambling urges us to trust in easy money as our salvation. I quote Verse 10 of our reading from I Timothy:

"For the love of money is the root of all evils; it is through this craving that some have wandered away from the faith and pierced their hearts with many pangs."

You may have heard the saying: "Money is the root of all evils." Well, notice that that is not what the Bible says. Rather it is: "the *love* of money is the root of all evils." Money is good; money is necessary. But, when we think that money is going to solve all our problems, when we crave more and more and more as our road to happiness and our security blanket, then we love money rather than God.

But the promoters of gambling paint a rosy, glitzy picture. I have here a brochure from Foxwoods; it shows pictures of people having fun: "Experience the largest casino in the entire world—the wonder of the Connecticut woods. Watch the sun set over the rolling hills as you join the action at hundreds of table games. ... The spotlight is always on exciting entertainment at Foxwoods. ... Satisfy your appetite in our tempting collection of restaurants. ... Discover a world of fascinating specialty shops. ..."

It sounds like a fun family outing, doesn't it? And, even our pro-gambling legislators promote gambling with promises that it will revitalize the economy with more jobs, with tax relief, that society will have no increase in crime, plus large benefits to education. But they don't tell us the negatives.

The owner of Bill's Joke and Novelty Shop in Brockton was quoted in the paper, saying that, "It is amazing how much people will spend on lottery tickets in a day; as much as $75." He went on to say that he has seen people spend their whole paychecks on the lottery. That money, then, does not go to the mortgage, or to rent, or to food, to savings for education, or to charity.

Another example of the negative side is Atlantic City. Since the casinos began there, retail business has dropped by one-third; the restaurant business has dropped by 40 percent. And, also, the promoters of gambling don't tell us about the social costs. More tax dollars are needed for police and emergency medical teams, to name two. And gambling is the fastest growing addiction among teenagers. Ninety-six percent of the country's 10 million compulsive gamblers got started before they reached the legal betting age.

Eddie Felton, "Fast Eddie," as he was called, was quite impressed when his father took him to the racetrack. His dad won every race he bet. As soon as Felton was old enough, he began to gamble. One time he took $100 to Foxwoods, and won $8,000. Having visions of becoming a millionaire, he ran through all of his credit cards, wrote rubber checks, and didn't even have enough money to make it home. The promises of gambling are empty promises.

Gambling has us in its grip. Again, the Bible says, "it is through this craving that some have wandered away from the faith and pierced their hearts with many pangs."

What is our response? Are we not the people of God, called to be the light of the world, witnesses for God? But, you might well say, "I can gamble because I'm not addicted. What harm is there? It is entertainment; it is excitement."

But, for a little entertainment, we are supporting that which is destructive to society. We are, in fact, our brother and sister's keepers. By personal lifestyle and social action we are called, as Timothy says, "to fight the good fight" of the faith, not just to satisfy our personal whim. You and I could influence someone else to gamble. We can waste the precious financial resources that God has given us. Timothy again speaks to us: "But as for you, man (woman) of God, shun all these things; aim at righteousness, godliness, faith, love, steadfastness, gentleness." These are qualities that enhance life for everyone.

The United Methodist Church's Social Principles also have an important word for us:

> Gambling is a menace to society, deadly to the best interest of moral, social, economic and spiritual life and destructive of good governments. ... Christians should abstain from gambling and should strive to minister to those victimized by the practice. ... The Church should promote standards and personal lifestyles that would make unnecessary the resort to commercial gambling - including public lotteries.

In Massachusetts, the casino was defeated in 1997. That is a testimony to the power of all the churches and others who have faithfully fought the battle. We can be sure that the battle is not over; it is always there.

Let me close with these thoughts. If you gamble, whether a little or a lot, think about it in relation to your understanding of God's word to you. Can you justify it by Scripture? If you need help freeing yourself from compulsive gambling, the church and others are here to help. And, to all of us, when elections come around, watch for the position that various candidates are taking on gambling expansion. And, always, speak out at every opportunity, in order to be helpful to others. Let us put our whole trust in God, whose promises are always dependable. Listen to these words from I Timothy 6:17, an apt summary for us today. (Do) "not set (our) hopes on uncertain riches but on God who richly furnishes us with everything to enjoy."

Afraid of Easter

Mark 16:1-8

Rev. Frances P. Swartz

This sermon was preached Easter Sunday, April 23, 2000 at Central United Methodist Church, Brockton, Mass. It is a first-person presentation of Mary Magdalene. The preacher wore a plain white robe, head covered with a scarf, to represent a first century Jewish woman.

GOOD MORNING! I am Mary Magdalene. I have been visiting your church and community, and would like to talk with you. You see, I know that you read the Easter story from Mark today, and I thought that you might be, well, shocked. You probably came to church today expecting to hear about how the women ran from the tomb to tell the disciples that Jesus is risen. Am I right? Is that what you expected? Well, I don't blame you at all for feeling disappointed when Mary Salome and I ran from the tomb in fright, and then said nothing to anyone. Yes, that's the sad truth. We did nothing! I'm not proud of it! But, I'd like for you to hear my side of the story. I am hoping that you will understand how we felt. This is what happened.

It has been a horrible week. Mary, Salome and I watched, as Jesus died an agonizing death on a cross. He meant the world to us! We watched as they placed him in a grave. In those days, we often used caves to bury our dead. The Sabbath was coming on, so he had to be buried quickly. My friends and I wanted Jesus to at least have a proper burial so, as soon as the Sabbath was over, we bought spices to anoint his body, according to Jewish custom. As soon as the sun rose on Sunday morning, we set off to go to his tomb. Now, I want you to picture this. As we approached the tomb, we saw that it was open. How would you have felt if that had been your loved one? They wouldn't even let him rest in peace! We tentatively stepped into the cave, and were shocked again to see someone, a young man, an angel maybe, I don't know. But he sat there in this white robe. Who was he? What did he want? What was going on? I'm glad that I wasn't alone! My friends and I huddled together for support. He told us not to be afraid. I guess he could see our jaws hanging and our knees knocking. He told us that Jesus had been raised from the dead and was not there in the tomb. Then he told us to go and tell the disciples and Peter that Jesus was going on ahead of us to Galilee. Galilee was our hometown area, like Brockton is for many of you. I'm telling you, we were in shock; we were overwhelmed! We ran; we were so terrified. I didn't have the courage to carry out that wonderful mission. Oh, believe me, I have thought about this; I have relived those moments over and over again. How I wish it had been different.

But, here's the other half of what I want to tell you; what about you? We failed to follow Jesus, but you don't have to! Do you know anyone who needs to know that Jesus is risen? Tell them! Please! Don't be afraid, as I was. Jesus is with you! Remember how the angel said, "He is going before you to Galilee." We were not to search for him on some mountaintop; all we had to do was to go home. Galilee was our home, just as Brockton or Easton is your home. And right here, Jesus will give you a ministry in his name.

I see you and other Christians doing so much. For example, I heard of a woman who was asked to be a Sunday schoolteacher. "Oh, I couldn't do that," she replied. Well, she overcame her fear and did such a great job that her church gave her an award. How about that?

Now, let's be honest. Are you afraid of Easter, just as I was? Are you wishing that you could just hear the story, and not have to do anything about it? Are you also afraid of following Jesus? I have learned a great deal about you in my visit here. You are so busy; I was never that busy in Galilee. You seem to be afraid to stop, to let go of your schedules and to go to church or to help someone. But there is another way that we are very much alike. You also seem to be afraid to venture out into something new. You love what is familiar. I understand that because, in my day, we women had our defined role. We didn't dare venture outside of it. But you have so much freedom and yet you are still, so often, afraid. I see young people staying in their groups in school; I see many communities of all one color and income level. Why don't people reach out beyond the ones who look and talk like them? It can be frightening to follow Jesus if it takes you beyond what is comfortable or even safe.

I have learned that you had a terrible anniversary this week, of two students killing other students and a teacher at a high school somewhere. We didn't have such violence among students in my day. No wonder many students today say they are afraid. There was one student, I heard about, named Rachel, who was asked by the killers if she believed in God. When she answered, "Yes," they killed her. I remember wondering, on that first Easter morning, if I followed him, would I have to die, too?

I heard about another student who overcame his fears. Richard Williams saw the television report of the tragedy. He was especially touched to hear of one of the students, whose name is Lance. Lance had been shot in the legs, and might never be able to participate in the sport of running again. Richard was a runner too, and he thought how terrible it would be not to be able to run. He decided that he would run for Lance, to raise money for his medical treatments. It started out to be a very small effort, until people began to hear about it. They wanted to participate too, and before he knew it, Richard had raised $18,000 in that race. Well, the contributions kept coming in until he raised $40,000. Richard then decided that he would deliver the money in person. So a black urban teenager traveled to meet a white suburban teenager. The two became fast friends, and they continue to keep in touch. Listen to what Richard said to the media. "I'm just a kid. If I can do that, there is no limit to what an adult can do."

Before I leave you, I want to assure all of you that there is no limit to what you and I can do, because Jesus Christ is alive and through him we can overcome our fears and accomplish great things for God. God bless you!

A Children's Sermon for Palm Sunday

Rev. Frances P. Swartz

HOW MANY OF you like parades? Today we are going to tell the story of a wonderful parade, the Palm Sunday parade. I am going to need you to help me with sound effects and motions. Let's practice first. When the story is happy, we're going to shout: "Hurray for Jesus!" Let's do it. (All shout, and wave their hands above their heads.) Good! Then, when our story is sad, we're going to hiss and frown. Let's do that. (All hiss and frown.) Good!

Now the story. Everyone in Jerusalem was all excited! Jesus was coming to town. ("Hurray for Jesus!") Everyone gathered, lining the streets on both sides—children, parents, grandparents. They were so excited to see Jesus riding into the city on a donkey. Some people took palm branches and waved them and others took off their coats and put them on the road while shouting: ("Hurray for Jesus!")

"Jesus has done such wonderful things," they said. "He has healed the sick, raised the dead, and from one boy's lunch he fed 5,000 people." ("Hurray for Jesus!") Everyone thought, Jesus is king of kings and lord of lords! ("Hurray for Jesus!")

But, there were some people in town who could only greet Jesus with a frown. (Hiss and frown.) "This Jesus, he's no king! We don't want him around!" (Hiss and frown.) It was true that Jesus didn't look like a king; he had no crown, BUT he loved everyone around! ("Hurray for Jesus!")

In a few days the sad thing was, some people put Jesus on a cross to kill him! (Show a palm cross or another type of cross.) It was a sad day, indeed, for everyone. It seemed as though his enemies had won the day. (Hiss and frown.)

But, three days later Jesus' friends saw him alive again! He promised to be with them after he went back up into the sky to God. He told his friends, "You have lots to do. Go and preach, baptize and heal. And remember, I am always with you!" ("Hurray for Jesus!")

Places in the Heart

Luke 24:35-48; I John 3:1-7; Acts 3:1-19

Rev. Dr. David A. Purdy

This sermon was preached at Crawford Memorial United Methodist Church, Winchester, Mass., April 21, 1985.

IT HAS RECEIVED so much publicity that even if you haven't seen the film "Places in the Heart," you probably have a rough idea of what it's about. It takes place on a farm in Southwest Texas during the Depression. The sheriff is called away from his family's dinner table to put down a disturbance. A young black man has a gun, is drunk, and is firing the gun at random and screaming incomprehensibly. The sheriff knows the man by name and as he approaches the man to take the gun away, the man accidentally fires it and kills the sheriff. The death leaves a wife and their two small children to run their farm alone. The bank is about to foreclose on the mortgage, when a black man wanders by looking for work. He seems knowledgeable about planting and picking cotton, and so she decides she will not only grow cotton, but also win the contest for the first farmer to bring the crop to market. In the meantime, the bank president has a blind brother-in-law who needs a place to stay and he figures that the widow could use the extra money that he would pay for his brother's lodgings.

In the end, of course, everyone contributes to the successful harvesting of the cotton, her winning the prize, and keeping the farm. However, the black man, who so ably assists her, is harassed by the Ku Klux Klan because it was his "uppityness" that helped her win. And so he must leave the farm.

Now, interestingly enough, the film begins in church with the strains from the hymn "Blessed Assurance" providing a kind of background music throughout the film. In the end, we are in church again. We see the people gathered, communion is being served and the congregation is singing, "Blessed assurance, Jesus is mine. Oh what a foretaste of glory divine." As the camera follows the bread being passed up and down the rows of people, we see first the hands of the people white and black assisting each other with the bread. Then the camera backs away and we see the sheriff sitting with his family; we see the man who had shot him and who had been lynched by the angry townspeople. Sitting next to him, the blind man and the children are there, and the black man who had been run out by the KKK. The sister and her estranged husband are sitting next to each other. The camera backs away further, out the church door and we see the little church from a distance surrounded by the fields of grain, while the screen fills to this broad picture, the chords of "Blessed Assurance" end with the words "watching and waiting, looking above, filled with his goodness, lost in his love."

People leaving the theater are puzzled by the ending. The rest of the film, though perhaps somewhat melodramatic, was realistic in its approach. But, now, here at the end, this note of surrealism is thrown in: all the people who had been killed, who had been separated and estranged from one another are all together in the church sharing in the bread and the cup, the body and blood of Christ. In all the reviews I have seen, both on TV and in the newspapers, I never noticed any critic making any comment at all about the ending, as though it were such an aberration that it couldn't be dealt with. How can the film end this way, with these people who are murdered, shot, divorced, abused ... all now sitting and singing and sharing together?

Though this is a good old-fashioned American story of the underdog who wins against nature and human odds, it is also set within a religious context; even more, it is a story of the resurrection. Not because the widow wins the prize and keeps the farm, and not because suddenly those who were dead and broken suddenly seem to have come back to life, but because the film is a film of hope; because it is saying there at the end in faith we shall all gather at the table of the Lord, we shall be restored to health and wholeness, we shall be renewed and reconciled. This is really a vision of the great eschatological banquet, when people are gathered from everywhere to sit at the table of the Lord.

Places in the heart ... the resurrection takes place in the heart, in the lives of people as they work and struggle and live together in the assurance of God's love. All of this may seem like nonsense, just as the end of the film seemed like nonsense, but it is the heart of the resurrection faith.

Now, I want to switch the scene, moving back in time from the sun-drenched field of 20th century Texas to the first century of the Common Era, to Jerusalem on the Friday of Passover week. Jesus, ridiculed as the King of the Jews, is hanging on a cross, the life draining from him as his lungs are caving in and breathing becomes more difficult. Finally as it grows toward noon, great clouds have covered the sun and it is dark, almost as dark as night. "Then the curtain in the Temple was torn in two from top to bottom. The earth shook, the rock split apart, the graves broke open, and many of God's people who had died were raised to life. They left their graves, and after Jesus rose from death, they went into the Holy City, where many people saw them." (Matt. 27:51-53).

Here's another story which ends nonsensically. It begins with a kind of crude realism; a real man is tried, convicted and suffers the pain of real execution. And then, suddenly, we are given the surrealistic scene of the ground shaking, the graves opening, the dead rising out of them, and the curtain of the Temple being torn in two.

What other way, I wonder, did the biblical writer have of portraying his belief that in the crucifixion of Christ something radical happened at the very heart of the universe? This was not your everyday execution, but the death of the Son of God at the hands of perverse people, and all of nature has gone haywire in response to this most catastrophic of circumstances.

But this is not just high surrealistic drama. Something important is being described. The curtain of the Temple is torn in two. The curtain had delineated the outer court of the Temple from the holy of holies. Only the priests could enter that special area behind the curtain, and then only on certain holy days after an elaborate purification ceremony. It was as if God was confined to that small place, held captive, as it were, by the elaborate ritual of the priests and their religious tradition. God, the Holy, by being liturgically honored in only one small space, was reserved for only the special, the privileged few. But when the temple curtain is ripped in two at the moment of Christ's death, God, as it were, escapes the narrow confines of that place. Everyone now has access to God, for God is no longer located in only one place, but God is free to lodge in the places of the heart.

Now, let's move the scene yet again; it is a few months earlier. We see Peter and several other friends of Jesus heal a man at the gate going into the temple. The healing is witnessed by those who are going in and out of the temple by that gate, especially since the man healed had become something of a local character. He had been lame since birth, and every morning friends would take him to the temple gate, to beg money from those who were entering the temple to make their offerings to God.

Temple authorities question Peter and the others on their ability and authority to heal. By what right and in whose name do they perform such miracles? "It was the God of your own fathers who is responsible for this healing," is the reply, "And in doing so God manifested the glory of his servant, Jesus." The disciples, the small early kernel of what was to become the church, is now the divinely appointed messianic community through which the God of Israel is now at work.

And the God of Abraham and Jacob and Jesus, who possesses this power to restore to health and wholeness the hurt and the broken, the poor and the outcast, acts not inside the temple precincts but outside its gates. God is no longer confined to the temple, held captive by the priests and other religious authorities. God is no longer confined to the sacred places ... to those places where someone or some special group of people have decided that, that's exclusively, the only place where God can function, and only for a particular group of people. As Jesus breaks the bonds of death, and the stone in front of the tomb is thrust aside, so God declares power and authority outside of the little narrow boxes in which we would attempt to hold him.

Easter, this marvelous "queen of seasons," as the hymn calls it so poetically, is not about dead bodies walking around; this isn't zombies on parade or something crass and bizarre like that. It is about the power of God to heal and reconcile and redeem the broken places in the heart.

And now, if you can, one more shift in scene. We are at a series of selectmen's and other town meetings where the issue of expanding the opportunities for low- and moderate-income housing is being discussed.

We hear adults counsel young people to carry baseball bats to protect themselves from the poor people who will move into and take over Winchester if the town adopts a broader housing policy than is currently in place. We hear lawyers, on behalf of concerned neighborhood groups, claim that the housing problem is really a fiction of governmental imagination. We hear concerned citizens express their desire to keep Winchester's character unchanged. These folk naturally have fears. They have themselves moved from the city to the suburb to find security and a country atmosphere for their children. They have much invested in their property and don't want to see its value diminished. They don't want to see high-density projects bring the troubles which they saw in the city to the country. But underneath the legitimate concerns and the concomitant fears, there is a vision. A vision of a place apart, a sacred place, if you will, where there are no elderly, no handicapped, no immigrants, no non-whites. A place where the temple still stands and its curtain remains intact. A place where God dwells exclusively to bless those of special privilege, those who can afford the temple tax and offerings, those who can by their strength and health, go through the beautiful gate of the temple and behind the temple's curtains, there to bend the knee to their exclusive God. Oh yes, they shall have to tolerate the lame beggar who seems always to be sitting just outside the gate, but they shall pacify him with a coin or two—he shall not get into their sacred confines, nor shall their God ever really be his. For he is their God and theirs alone, and they are his people, his alone.

Such may be a Utopian vision for the few who by health, luck, family background, education and hard work have access to it. But it is not a vision of the resurrection. As people who believe in the resurrection, we know that God has ripped that temple curtain in two, that the beggar at the gate is healed not so that he can now have access to the exclusive arena of the holy of holies, but because our God's power and love extends far behind the holy place, making every place holy. As people of the resurrection we have a utopian vision too—one against all the odds we must continue to lift up and live before. A vision of all God's people living and working and struggling and suffering and rejoicing and celebrating together! Of people with different backgrounds, age, skin color, skills and income enhancing one another's lives! A place where there are no baseball bats carried for protection but hands extended, inviting a diversity of God's people whereby everyone's life can be enriched!

As the messianic community embodying the resurrected Christ, we believe in and affirm the utterly nonsensical and absurd vision of all God's people serving one another the bread and the cup, sitting and singing together: "Blessed assurance, Jesus is mine! O what a foretaste of glory divine! Heir of salvation, purchase of God, born of his Spirit, washed in his blood." Amen.

Go Kiss a Frog

Romans 5:1-11

Rev. Dr. David A. Purdy

This sermon was preached at Crawford Memorial United Methodist Church, Winchester, Mass., Nov. 25, 1979.

THE THREE YOUNG women, one a schoolteacher, the other two members of the youth fellowship, were on their way to the church that Christmas Eve to get ready for their participation in the quiet pageantry of that most wonderful of celebrations. They were not late, on time for once they joked to one another, so they were not speeding. But the young man who'd spent the whole afternoon going from one bar to another was speeding. Suddenly, the serenity of that crystal clear Christmas Eve exploded as his car plowed head-on into the young women.

We came upon the accident a few minutes after it had taken place. I recognized the car and asked the policeman how badly people had been hurt. The man is dead, the three girls are still alive, but they're in bad shape. He did not know who they were. I told him I did and that I would notify their families. We continued down toward the church, calling hospital and families when we arrived. The service that followed a few minutes later was a prayerful and subdued one. There was none of the misty-eyed joy of Christmas Eve that night.

When I got to the hospital, two of the girls had been tended to. When the blood had been wiped away, it was discovered that their injuries, miraculously, were rather minor. A concussion, a few stitches, a twisted ankle. But the young schoolteacher had been taken to a larger, better-equipped hospital in a nearby city. When I asked the nurse how bad the situation looked, she grimaced and her brief words gave little hope.

I could not see her that evening. She was in surgery the whole night, but the next morning when I went into intensive care; she looked like some monster from a grade-B movie. Her jaw had been wired together with stainless steel and she would be unable to open her mouth for three months. Her broken legs were in casts, one hung from the gleaming framework that surrounded her bed. Her face was purple and misshapen from the bruises; later, I would see the stitches that ran the length of her torso. There were wires running from her chest to the monitoring device above her bed; there were tubes dripping life-sustaining fluids into her body; and tubes, three of them, coming out of her nose pumping dark fluids from her body. Oddly enough she was awake, and according to the medical team attending her, she seem lucid ... though she could not speak because her mouth was clamped shut by the wires holding her jaw in place.

As I approached her bed, the few well-rehearsed lines I had been practicing on the way up to the hospital room fled my mind forever. For I stood before a person who was more machine than flesh and blood, a person who could not speak or smile, whose eyes revealed shock and fright. I managed a modicum of composure, I muttered a few inane words; I groped under the sheet to touch her hand only to find it, too, wrapped in white bandages. I offered prayer, followed by the Lord's Prayer. When I looked at her, revulsion and nausea began to overcome me again. Was she alive or dead; was she a woman or a machine; what would become of her, her young husband who was out of work, her mother and father, her 95-year-old grandmother? Those thoughts, the smell of antiseptic, the glaring lights, the whiteness of the sheets and casts, the tubes and hoses and glistening steel began to make my head swim.

It was a dream, a nightmare; it couldn't be real; I wanted to wake up, and failing that, to run away. But I stayed, just a few moments more, for out of this nightmare scene a voice seemed to be directing me. Every part of her body was wrapped in plaster or bandages, virtually every part of her body had been injured, but I pushed away the hoses taped to her forehead and moved the tubes alongside the bed, and I leaned over, and kissed her forehead.

As I turned to go, her eyes began to moisten and she blinked as if in some kind of code language that she had been developing in her few waking hours. Her face relaxed, and through it all I felt a "thank you" being communicated. She had become a person again. Before school was out that spring, she was back teaching, learning to use her new teeth and testing her torn ligaments and still nursing some sore spots and covering a few scars. The church had raised money to help with the hospital bills and a new car. When she could receive visitors, they went in droves; the young group organized car pools to make sure someone was there all the time.

Four years later, she would be back in the hospital again. She needed three feet of intestine removed to get rid of scar tissue and adhesions which had built up on her old injuries. The hoses and tubes would be back, for a while following surgery. This time, though, she could talk and write. And this is part of a letter she wrote to the church people:

> My dear friends,
>
> I have just finished looking thru (sic) my fast growing pile of get well cards. I had to ask my nurse to let me borrow some paper and a pen. How can I ever thank you enough for all your kind thoughts and messages and prayers? To feel the strength and love flowing out from all of you and thru (sic) you to Christ. All human fellowships suffer thru (sic) their ups and downs, but how comforting to know that Christ's fellowship - the church - is stilling going on as strong as always despite human frailties. Your love and care is more important to me than you will ever know.
>
> THANK YOU ALL!
>
> Love and fellowship,
>
> Linda

What kept her from becoming bitter and cynical; what had reinforced her faith in God and her love for the church? It was, she would say later, that she had been held and touched in prayer and in person by the people of that church: "I was feeling like that ugly monstrous frog in the fairy tale, over whose life a spell had been cast by some wicked witch. My transformation began the night you came and prayed with me, but more than that, when you kissed me. I began to feel beautiful and whole again."

As this courageous woman's life reveals, there is more spiritual truth than make believe in that old fairy tale. There are a lot of people in this world, and not a few in our churches, who for one reason or another feel like ugly, "froggy" people. Whether it is a physical infirmity, or emotional stress, or spiritual crisis, they are frightened, they are alienated, they experience isolation; they feel the lack of love. And the only way for them to be transformed—to become a handsome prince or pretty princess again—is to see the potential beneath the "froggy" green, warty skin and to kiss them into their inheritance.

It's nice to be a frog kisser when you know how the story is going to come out in the end. It makes you feel good to know that you had some hand in helping a person look at their life in a different, more wholesome way. But frog kissing can be a pretty risky business too. There is always the danger that the frog will stick its tongue out at you as though you were just one more bug on its menu, someone whose love and generosity is devoured, but which has no magical, transforming effect. You and I both know that there seem to be as many people who are hardened against God by tragedy as there are those who turn to God for healing, help and wholeness in their vulnerability. A young boy died in our parish one year, and the father, in his grief and his guilt, grew into a hard and bitter man. After the funeral, he never came to church again. I would see him walk past our house day after day on his way to work, his teeth clenched, his eyes looking straight ahead, his body rigid. I tried to reach out to him; I invited him to lunch. I hoped to get him to talk about it. I tried to be close—but only for a while, for his look was menacing, and, frankly, he frightened me. It never occurred to me that the fear he engendered in me must have been the fear he lived with every day. The wall he built around himself was his way of keeping the wicked witch of life from ever pricking him again. And I gave up on him. His ugliness drove me away. I live daily with that guilt, with the possibility that I might have been God's instrument for healing and that I "chickened out." I also live with the knowledge that I am only human, that I am not the redeemer. Yet, if the frog hides behind his ugliness, we must continue to be vulnerable to that ugliness. We must continue to bend, and to touch, and to hope and to kiss.

Sometimes it's the frog that objects to our handling. Like the father of the dead boy, he says to us: "I'm poison; touch me and you'll get warts too. I like being miserable. I don't want to be a prince, because once you're a prince again, you're vulnerable to the pricks of life. And so, I'm determined to stay a miserable frog, because I just can't take any more chances on being disappointed again. And the more people I can drag with me, the more miserable we can all be. ... We can sit around on the edge of the pond all day croaking about the hypocrisy of the people who are trying to kiss us and who finally give up."

Sometimes the pressure not to kiss a frog comes from the others around us who have, indeed, given up, who say, "forget it, that's one lost cause." Or from others who are so dignified that they could never pick up a frog and kiss it. But, thank God, there are those willing to run the risk of rebuff and ridicule. For there is no other way that this ugly "froggy" world will be redeemed. For under the warts is the image of God. Under the hard and ugly skin is a person aching for release ... a prince or princess in disguise.

It is not the fairy tale that informs us in these matters, though, because at the end of the fairy tale everyone lives happily ever after. Our life pattern is that of Jesus Christ, who is described in the words of the Apostle Paul: "... though he was in the form of God, he did not count equality with God a thing to be grasped, but emptied himself, taking the form of a servant, being born in the likeness of men." (Philippians 2:6-7).

He is the one who heals, and we represent him in his holy work when we become his followers, when we become servants, vulnerable to the spit and spears of the frogs. Christ it was who washed dirty feet and forgave his tormentors, who sat with sinners and who hugged the leper.

As we celebrate this last Sunday in the season of Kingdomtide, before we begin the Christian year again with Advent next week, we would do well to remember that God's kingdom comes, and the reign of God is recognized, every time a frog is turned into a prince/princess. Jesus' final words to his disciples in Matthew's Gospel are these: "All authority in heaven and earth has been given to me. Go, therefore, and make disciples of all nations ... and lo, I am with you always, to the end of the age." Until the kingdom shall be fully realized.

In kissing frogs, Christ released the royalty in each one of us; we are, St. Paul wrote, " A royal priesthood, God's own people."

In the New International Version of the Bible, the translator puts Paul's words we read in Romans this morning this very graphic way: "Very rarely will anyone die for a righteous man, though for a good man someone might possibly dare to die. But God demonstrates his love for us in this: that while we were yet spitting on him, Christ died for us."

That seems to me to be the ultimate in kissing frogs. And it has proven time and time again to be the only way that the spell that the wicked witch casts over us can be broken. If for us, then also for others. With apologies only to Kermit the Frog, be a prince or princess, one of God's royal kingdom citizens, and go kiss a frog this week.

On Violence

John 10:1-10

Rev. Shirley S. Hoover

This sermon was preached at St. John's United Methodist Church, Dover, N.H., April 25, 1999, the Sunday after the Columbine High School shooting of students and teachers by two fellow students. The sermon manuscript is presented in the format used by Rev. Ms. Hoover, one which helps compensate for a vision problem. However, the font size used here is smaller than in the original preaching manuscript.

Somewhere I read that good preaching comes from
holding the Bible in one hand
and a newspaper in the other.

So I come this morning with the Bible and the newspaper.

By now everyone must know about the two high school boys,
whose minds were twisted by some deep
and unfathomable rage,
who plotted and planned, we now know for almost a year,
to kill as many classmates as they could
and to destroy their school.

It sounds like a bizarre story of horror dreamed up by some Hollywood flack,
but it is a true story of horror and terror,
played out on the television screen for all the world to see.

The global village writ large on our psyches.

We turn to the newspaper to find some answers
and to make some sense of this terrible evil
that occurred at Columbine High School in Littleton, Colorado
last week.

The Boston Globe, April 23, 1999, published an opinion column on the front page written by Eileen McNamara and headlined: "Not a time to flinch from the questions."

She writes:

> School uniforms will not fix what has gone wrong in America, but already we are seizing on such facile solutions in the aftermath of the massacre this week at Columbine High School.
>
> Instead of addressing the need for stricter gun controls and better outreach services to alienated adolescents, we are talking about dress codes, video games and rock 'n' roll lyrics. Like every act of violence, the slaying of 12 students and a teacher by two disaffected teenagers is a reflection of the culture in which it occurred. Our children play out apocalyptic fantasies on their computer screens. They listen to the suicidal seductions of self-styled "death rockers." They line up for tickets to movies marketing horror and mayhem expressly to them.
>
> Most of our children, however, do not spend their weekends at dad's workbench fashioning bombs out of propane tanks from the backyard grill. Most do not stroll into school on a sunny spring morning, toting sawed-off shotguns and semiautomatic rifles under their long black coats.
>
> Why, then, did the two presumed killers Eric Harris, 18, and Dylan Kiebold, 17??...."

Her question is the one we always ask when something terrible happens: Why?

And as I have listened to the TV
and read the papers
and talked and listened to various people during this week
one of the things I have heard is
what we always do when tragedy occurs.
We want to fix the blame.
We are willing to place the blame almost anywhere
except where the responsibility truly lives.

We blame it on the media,
the music kids listen to these days,
the parents,
the schools,
our lack of moral values,
the breakdown of the family,
not enough security in the schools,
too easy availability of guns.

And probably all of the above must share the blame.
But that is not all there is.

On Friday, I also received an e-mail from several people.
I'm on a lot of lists I have discovered.

This e-mail suggested
that people drive with their lights on this weekend
to show support for the families of those injured or killed
last Tuesday in Colorado.

I thought that seemed like a good idea
and then I read the message a little more carefully —
and thought a little more deeply about it
for the message said:

"Light up America, show that you care about
what is right about our country."

But a part of what is wrong in this country right now and in the past actually is our failure.

Indeed,
our determination is to see only what is right with America
and not to see the dark side of America
that is omnipresent and just as real.

We want to proclaim what is right with America;
we want to ignore what is not right with America.

Please hear me say what I am trying to say.
I am not comparing this country to any other country.

I am talking about the nation that is mine,
the nation that I know
because I have been a citizen
for what is getting to be a long time.

I am talking about the country that I love.

But there is a dark side to our national character.
And our efforts to ignore it are beginning to bear a terrible fruit
For what we are seeing increasingly, too often, is
the eruption into national life of a dark side
that won't stay hidden any longer.

As a nation we tend to be generous,
adventurous,
creative,
inventive,
willing to risk
and, most of the time, trying to stand for justice.

But we are also a people of violence.
We have been since the beginning of our history
  when we pushed the native peoples off their land
  and kept pushing until they fought back
    and then we very nearly destroyed them.

We have dealt with the land itself violently,
  cutting down forests and plowing and planting
    without regard for the effect on the soil
      because we were so big
  and there was plenty more forest and good topsoil
  and clean water —
    just a little further west.

So we created a dust bowl,
  and then later we strip-mined the land and clear-cut the woods,
  and polluted the water and the air
    as if this land was ours to destroy
    and not God's creation blessing us with abundance.

The frontier for a long time acted as a kind of safety valve
  where all the violent people could kill each other off,
  and in the absence of law and justice they did.

And civilized people did not have to bother about outlaws
  and renegades and thieves.

Lynching is a part of our history.
Racism of every kind is a part of our history.
Suspicion and hatred of the stranger,
  of the one who is different,
  are a part of our history
  as any immigrant from the past or the present can tell you.

In our time that hatred erupts in racial brutality
  and gay-bashing even unto death.

Now we have "road rage,"
where angry people use their cars as weapons to terrorize
other drivers on the road.
If you have not been the target of it yet,
you have an experience coming!

And then, there are our guns,
the ones we keep in our homes to do violence
to those who would do violence to us.

And the guns we keep for hunting and sport shooting.

And, then, there is the ready availability
of semi-automatic guns of every kind
whose only purpose, as far as I can see, is to kill people.
The homes of too many of us are not safe,
for there is something we now call domestic violence.

It is nothing new, but not too long ago we paid no attention to it,
because a man's home was his castle
and what went on in it was nobody's business.

Now, we have raised up generation after generation
of physically abused children and women and elderly
— and, to be fair, occasionally, men.
We raised them up to continue the violence in their families.

But there is more than physical abuse that can kill the body,
there is verbal abuse that can kill the soul.
The put-downs,
the criticism,
the name calling,
degrading and demeaning attitudes toward others,
humiliation,
language that destroys self-esteem,
and words that hurt and stunt and diminish

all are another expression of the dark side of our national character.

Even while we deny and try to pretend
that this dark side of our national character doesn't exist,
we give it tacit approval.

We regard murder and shooting and maiming and blood and gore
as entertainment on the TV in our homes,
in the films we pay to see.

We condone official violence when it is done by the police,
in the name of law and order,
or when the state takes a life through capital punishment.

Too many of us are willing to take a life,
before it even begins,
through abortion.

And let me name it for what it is, the greatest violence of all is war.

The juxtaposition last week of pictures of the damage wrought by
bombs in Belgrade and other places in Yugoslavia,
and long lines of frightened refugees
fleeing their homeland for their very lives,

and the pictures of SWAT teams and bloody school children
was almost beyond comprehension and sense.

And that list of our violent ways is only what I can think of quickly
off the top of my head.

I left out gang wars,
and kids playing cowboys and Indians and cops and robbers,
although I guess nowadays
they do it with pretend semi-automatic weapons.

Had enough? Heard enough?

Let me ask if there is any wonder
that there are those among us who can be susceptible to
and overwhelmed by the dark side of our character?

And the let me say that I am piling it up on purpose,
because I want us to see it;
I want us to feel it.
I want us to own it.
Because the dark side,
the violence does not belong to somebody else.

It belongs to us. We are responsible.

We who consider ourselves good Christian people,
participate in our violent culture just like everybody else.

And I know you would rather not own it.
I know that from the many conversations I had this week.

I know that because I would rather not own it either.

But until we do, horrors like what happened this week
will continue to happen in other affluent suburbs
and small towns and cities,
and maybe one day, God forbid, even in Dover.

Until we can recognize the ways
in which we participate in the violence,
it will continue to erupt among us in unexpected times and places.
Until we can recognize the ways we participate in the violence,
we can not even begin to change anything.
Until we are able to recognize the ways we participate in the violence,
all the security gates and uniformed police in the schools,
all the gun control laws,

all the censorship of films and TV we might undertake
will make no difference.

Until we can recognize that the only way to deal with what is evil,
and hurtful,
and destructive
is to bring it into the light where we can see it
and begin to acknowledge our part in it.

Anything else we do will be ineffective.

In the sublime way in which God's grace is given to us,
the children of Columbine High School,
who have looked so closely into the face of evil
have shown us the way.

They have learned that the only way to deal with evil and violence
is to turn to God.

I think I will never forget the faces of those grieving children,
as they began to find refuge and comfort
and the beginning of healing in their churches
that first night after the tragedy
which had changed their lives forever.

And they know it.

So much for the newspaper part of this sermon.

Here comes the Bible part.

If we are to change the climate of violence
in which our world is submerged,
and I believe we can —
indeed, I believe we must;

we, too, must turn to the good shepherd,
to Jesus the Christ,
to find in him the way which he offers us.

The first thing we must do is to look at our lives and behavior
in comparison to what we profess to believe
as followers of Jesus Christ.

Someone has said we live in a pre-Christian era,
as if we have never heard of Jesus Christ and his way.

But we *have* heard of him, we claim to be saved by him.
We claim to be children of God,
but too often we don't act as those who seek to do God's will.

So, perhaps, because we love Jesus
and truly want to follow him
and know that we are saved by his grace,

we can begin to own and name the culture of violence
that surrounds us.

If we are to truly be the Christians we are called to be,
we can resolve not to participate in this culture of violence
any longer or in any way that can be avoided.

And that change needs to begin right now.

By naming the dark side of our culture, change has begun.

More change could mean choosing not to see movies
that are filled with violence.

For me that means no more Robert de Niro films;
I enjoy his performances because he is so good at his craft
and I enjoy the plot of a good mystery action movie,

ignoring and not seeing how many people have been
killed before the film is finished.

I have seen my last de Niro film. I will not do that again.

And if my intention is to be fruitful,
I will write a letter to the actor, the producer and the film
company stating why I will no longer participate in that kind
of violence.

Changing the dark side of our culture could mean
examining our prejudices and hatreds,
naming and owning them,
forgiving ourselves and those who have hurt us,
accepting God's mercy and grace and resolving to sin no
more.

Changing the dark side of our culture,
we can choose to watch the words we use
and the damage that words can do.

We can cease to use our tongues as weapons;
we can begin a self-regulated tongue control,
and let phrases like:
"I could kill her" or "You are so stupid"
disappear from our vocabulary.

As parents we can monitor what our children do,
what films and TV they see,
what games they play.

If we don't do it, who will?

We can be careful what punishment we use.
Spanking is a form of violence,
although I heard that denied just yesterday by someone

who is a good Christian woman —
except maybe in this one area.

We can actually do what we say we do —
treat everyone with respect for their dignity and their worth
as children of God.

Not just those who look like us,
or speak like us,
or live in our neighborhood.

When Jesus said, "Love thy neighbor," he made no exceptions.
He meant *all* thy neighbors.

We can value ourselves as God's people,
called to be a light to the nations
called to be the body of Christ,
the hands and feet and voice of God in the world.

It begins with cleaning up our own act,
and then supporting efforts to find ways
to identify the twisted minds among us
before the disaster happens.

It begins with seeking way to help parents be better parents.
That is not a skill that comes naturally.
We have to *learn* how to do it well.

It begins with supporting ways to limit our currently easy access to weapons of all kinds.

It may require some regulation of what goes on the Internet.

It may require, for a while anyway,
limiting some of the freedoms we so cherish
for the good of the community,

so that our freedom is not limited by terror and abuse.

These last are but temporary measures to hold us
until the day when our hearts no longer
hide the dark side of our nature—except maybe in this one area.

In the meantime, we can keep our car lights on as a symbol,
not of what is right with America,
but as a sign of hope that America can be better.

We can heed the words of Isaiah,
"And a little child shall lead then,"
and follow the example of children.

The WWJD bracelet seems such a simplistic response,
but what better can we all do
than ask ourselves in all the situations of our lives,
"what would Jesus do?" and do it!

The ,good shepherd calls his sheep,
and the sheep follow him because they know his voice.

Too many of us have been seduced
by the dark side of our national character.

It is time to truly follow the voice of the one
whom we know loves us and promises us
that he came so that we might have life and have it abundantly.

We are the people of a God
who calls us to choose blessing or curse,
life or death. Let us choose life, and live accordingly.

Outsiders Brought In

John 4:5-26

Rev. Shirley S. Hoover

The style of this sermon is a modified version of guided imagery, often used by this preacher, and was first preached at Lee Memorial United Methodist Church, Norwich, Conn., March 14, 1993.

THIS SAMARITAN WOMAN, who is not named, has always been one of my favorite biblical characters. I have found it fruitful to try to step into her life, to walk a way in her shoes. So this morning I want to invite you to step into her sandals. I think she has something to teach us which may best be learned by trying to stand in her place for a few minutes. I invite you to come with me and participate in her life, as I describe it.

She is an outsider. As a Samaritan, she had no standing in the world of the Jews. Indeed, her people were deeply hated and regarded as little better than dogs. To get into her sandals, think about a time when you have felt like a stranger at some gathering or party. A time when you did not know anyone who was there! Or an occasion when you have felt hostility directed at you by others. She is an outsider, also, because she has had a number of husbands. This makes her unwelcome among her own people. Now think of a time when you have felt out of step with what everyone else is doing, when you felt quite isolated.

She is outside because she is a woman. She has no power whatsoever. Indeed, she is regarded as little better than property. She simply doesn't count. Now think about a time when your presence was ignored, a situation in which you felt as if you were not even "there." If you are female, it is not hard to remember such a situation. It happens all the time. If you are male, it will be a little harder, but try. Now you have a little sense of the loneliness and isolation that this woman experienced as part of her daily life. That loneliness and isolation were strong enough to persuade her to come to the well in the heat of the day, when she thought no one else would be there.

Now, I invite you to think a little about thirst. The land of Israel is a dry and arid place where water is scarce. Since water is essential to life, the scarcity also makes it precious. There were few wells or springs. Towns and villages were located near them. The well in the story has a long and ancient history. Here in New England there is an abundance of water. We are surrounded by a wonderful variety of plants and trees that the water supply supports.

I think it is hard for us to think about the kind of dryness and thirst that goes with a scarcity of water. Thirst takes on a greater significance when the distance between the sources of water is great, when you can't just go to the nearest faucet and get a drink. However, stretch yourself to think about being thirsty. Your mouth is dry, beginning to feel like cotton. Your skin is dry. As your thirst deepens you begin to feel parched, shriveled and diminished. It is hard to think about because we seldom allow ourselves to get that thirsty. Try to remember what thirst feels like and then imagine that there isn't any immediate source of liquid.

Now, maybe you can get a sense of what it is to be the Samaritan woman: lonely, isolated, cut off from community, thirsty of soul as well as body. "Give me that living water," she says, "and then I shall not be thirsty nor have to come all this way to draw water again."

When we try to get into the Samaritan woman's situation, we also enter into the current condition of many people in our contemporary society. They are lonely: separated from family and friends, whether by death, or divorce, or estrangement, or geographical distance. They are isolated, cut off from real community, thirsty of soul. Oh, so thirsty of soul. And they seek desperately for something that will slake the thirst, except that too many don't know that it is their soul that is thirsty. Even more, they don't know where the well is.

Spiritual search is partly what fuels the frantic pace at which we seem to be living these days. Always there are people on the road going somewhere, almost always faster than the posted speed limit. (I am an offender there.) Always there are crowds of people in the malls, at restaurants, at sports events, at the theater. We hurry to get in and we hurry to get out. We can get three-minute lunches, drive-up banking and drive-through food. Sometimes I wonder why the rush? And I get annoyed with myself when I realize that I am caught up in it, because I don't really need to search for the living water for my thirsty soul. I know where the well is.

I think the busyness and rapid pace is contagious because we do forget that what our thirsty soul longs for is God. Some of us think that we can slake our thirst with the consumption of material goods, so we accumulate things, most of which go well beyond necessity. In a peculiar kind of way, advertising tells us that this or that product meets our every need. Sometimes the commercials tell us this or that beer, or this or that deodorant will bring us the community we long for, or ease our loneliness, as well as quench our thirst. Sometimes the commercials even use the language and images of faith and community. And we believe what we hear and see. It takes us a long time to realize that all the possessions and things that we own do nothing to ease our yearning for God. Indeed, some never do figure it out.

And so, we occupy ourselves with empty pursuits and find that we are too busy for God. There's not enough time for worship, for prayer, for study of the Scriptures, for contemplation, for caring for others. These activities, which actually would ease our thirst, are on the bottom of our priority list. Apparently those of us who are older have forgotten where the well is. Our young never knew, so we wander, no, we run, frantically, parched and dry wondering to ourselves, when we pause for a moment, why we feel so unfulfilled, bored, negative, unhappy, wondering why the world doesn't measure up to our expectations, wondering: "Is this all there is?"

That is the question that expresses spiritual thirst. "Is this all there is?"

There are many, many people outside these walls who are spiritually thirsty. You'll find them today at the mall, or in front of the TV set, or in some other way numbing themselves to the emptiness of their lives. There are more than a few inside these walls who are spiritually thirsty, perhaps, more painfully so since they know they are thirsty, but they cannot quite bring themselves to the well.

What about this well near the ancient village of Sychar? Jesus makes it clear that this ancient well of Jacob, which has supported life in this desert for centuries, is not enough. Jesus says that he, Jesus, is the source of living water. He is the well we seek. It is through him that we can find life. And he teaches us that we are dependent upon God for all we need. All this frantic running around gains us nothing. He shows us what really matters in this life are loving and caring for our neighbor. The accumulation of things doesn't do it. Loving and caring for our neighbor is what fills us, eases our thirst, and makes us the source of living water for others.

Strange, isn't it, that this is so simple? Gaining life from this well doesn't require wealth; it does require time. It does require a concern for justice, and an understanding of what God cares about most. It doesn't require power. There is no way we can demand or force what God gives us freely. It does require faith that God's grace and mercy can and does move through us, that we are the conduit through which the living water comes. I've often said that this Samaritan woman was the first woman preacher. She was so effective as preacher that when she went to tell her neighbors about this messiah she had met at the well she brought back the whole town!

Obviously, she spoke to their thirst. She could speak with authority for her thirst had been satisfied. That's how it is with us, too, I suspect. When we can receive the grace of God and know that we are thirsty no more, then we are able to share that grace with others who need it. This is really a strange story in one sense. All sorts of barriers are broken. Jesus talked with a woman, a Samaritan, a despised person whose private life is irregular even for her time. This woman really enters into dialogue with him, thoughtful theological dialogue. Her separation is overcome, she is included in God's community.

Through her we discover that we, too, are included. Our loneliness and thirst eased, as we are drawn to the well of living water, the source of real life which is Jesus Christ. We can try to find the water that gives us life in any place under the sun. We can try to use substitutes, but there is only one true source of living water, only one wellspring of eternal life ... which is Jesus Christ himself.

For Natalie et al

Luke 24:1-12

Rev. Dr. William C. Coleman

This sermon was preached at Calvary Church United Methodist, Arlington, Mass., Easter Sunday, April 12, 1998.

IT WAS AN unlikely place and time. There we were, Natalie and I, installing sheet rock to cover a newly framed closet, preparing for the plasterer. Our younger daughter, Natalie, in her mid-30s, a parent herself, is characteristically straightforward. Commenting on conversations she had been having recently with some of her peers who are ill, or who have loved ones with terminal illness, she put it flat out: "Dad, do you believe in life after death? What do you really think?" I felt myself suck in a deep breath and think "oh-oh"; my preacher mind began to race through data looking for how to respond. My response, it shames me to say, was hesitant. I recall mumbling something like, "Well, yes, I do. But it is a bit complex to say why I believe in life after death." I think I said something further like, "I believe what Scripture says, because I can't see what would be in it for the disciples to fabricate a story about Jesus' resurrection if they didn't experience 'something' of Jesus being alive again."

Very inadequate, Natalie! So, now that I've had time to sort through my thoughts and experience, I want to see if I can give you and any others who care to listen a more complete and honest response to what I think about resurrection, life after death. However, I want you to know and trust that whatever I say to you about my belief is not and never can be a substitute for your own process of coming to terms with what you believe about life after death. At best, I am suggesting and pointing to some signposts that can move us through a thorny thicket. I believe I have glimpsed a way out, and have scouted out some paths that can fruitfully lead us up the mount of hope. At least I will try.

I think what you're asking me is, "When I die, what will happen to me? Will I be all right?" Or another way of framing this question, slightly less personally, is: "Is the Easter story true?" Let me juxtapose those questions with a comment made in the Easter account in Luke, when the women came to the disciples announcing that Jesus' burial tomb was empty, implying that Jesus is alive. The disciples' initial response is characterized this way: "These words seemed to them an idle tale, and they did not believe them." So in some ways, we may begin just about where most of the original disciples began. Later, the Scriptures share a variety of reports, experiences and affirmations by the disciples which declare that they met the resurrected Jesus. The "idle tale" is experienced to be true! However, what confuses some folk and frankly fosters doubt in many thinking people is that the reports of Jesus' resurrection vary, or at least the language of reporting varies, and the language used is poetic, symbolic and not very scientific. So how can these reports be reliable, even if well intended?

Well, the fact is that many things are mysterious, beyond the realm of ordinary experience, and we resort to poetry and symbols to talk about things we believe are there even though they are mysterious, cannot be seen or touched. Take quarks, for instance. As I understand it, physicists tell us quarks are hypothetical (no one has seen a quark), sub-atomic electric particles that are the building blocks of all matter, anything that occupies space. The bench you are sitting on begins with quarks. The word "quark" was coined by James Joyce the novelist in his book *Finnegan's Wake (Three quarks for Mr. Marks)* and physics took the word to refer to atomic particles which are the foundations of the universe. One physicist, when asked how these quarks interact with each other so as to draw near and adhere with each other to form matter, said: "The quarks charm one another." Charm? Yes, charm. What kind of scientific language is that? Well, let's not be too hard on the scientists. Often, to describe something, some phenomena, we are required, forced even, to resort to the imprecise language of symbol and poetry to try and say what we mean. There is no other way.

So in Scripture, when it says Jesus passes through a locked door to be among them following his resurrection, this is poetic language being used to describe the mysterious presence of Jesus, present with them after his death. On another occasion two people walking to Emmaus, shortly after the crucifixion, meet a stranger who walked along with them. The two people continued to discuss the hurt, the pain, and the disappointment they felt about losing Jesus to death through crucifixion. And, then, when they stopped for supper, the stranger was invited to eat with them. It was during the breaking of bread he, Jesus, became recognizable to them. They met the living Christ. They told others. And so it goes.

In our own family we have an account of your Great Grandmother Coleman experiencing the risen Christ. I never knew her, as she died several years before my birth. My mother, her daughter-in-law, cared for my grandmother during her last illness, a stroke, which left her speechless and partially paralyzed. Always a devout Methodist, my grandmother had lived well, raising a brood of nine children to adulthood. In the last hours of her life, Grandmother's breathing was labored, and she was unconscious. Several of her children were present at her bedside including my mother who reported to me the account. Never regaining consciousness to speak to her family, Grandmother, nevertheless, raised herself up to a sitting position, and with arms outstretched, radiant face, exclaimed, "Jesus." Then she fell back on the bed dead.

My mother was not raised in a practicing religious family, although she had been baptized Christian in her early teens. In John Wesley's terms, my mother at the point of Great Grandmother Coleman's death was an almost Christian. But she reported to me that from that moment, she never again questioned the validity, the reality of Jesus' resurrection. She became a convinced and practicing Christian. So, Natalie and others, part of what I believe is built upon the report of guides, whom I regard as reliable after long years of studying the Scriptures and wrestling with their witness. Their story, their narrative, their poetic language about their experience of the resurrection convinces me, steadies my faith that Jesus returned from the dead. It was an event totally out of the ordinary, obviously. He was known and recognized, even though the reports vary considerably about the exact forms that took.

I have come to accept the reliability of the Christian tradition, which forms much of my faith and hope regarding life after death—a process not unlike, I suppose, the one in which I accept the reliability of modern physics which tells me that sub-atomic particles, unseen, called quarks, are "charmed" by one another and come together to form the building blocks of all things. To do that, something which I can barely understand in the physical world, like with the resurrection, is a leap of faith, although I hope a thoughtful, carefully considered and informed leap of faith.

But, I would not want you to conclude that I believe in life after death only because I believe what others have told me, or have read about in Scripture, or have reasoned out for myself. That is all-important, of course. But there is more. For I, too, have discovered, as the first disciples of Jesus did, that God's gift of Jesus—his life, teachings, crucifixion, and resurrection—have kept me hopeful and alive in the midst of deaths and losses. I have experienced a kind of resurrection in this life before my physical death. I see the same thing in others as well. I have journeyed to cemeteries to bury members of my own family, friends and parishioners. I know you have, too. You have lost family members, friends, peers in deaths that in some instances seemed untimely. In my case, and in the case of people near my age or older, I suppose it is not uncommon to experience loss by death a dozen or so times before we die ourselves. By simple attrition we become the older generation and entertain from time to time thoughts about our own mortality, our own dying. What I am saying here is probably true of nearly all people. Some people, of course, faced with such losses become embittered, discouraged, fearful, lose hope, and do not creatively live fully again. The loss overwhelms them. One person, writing of a life in a concentration camp, reported that:

> "The most ghastly moment of the 24 hours of camp life was the awakening when, at a still nocturnal hour, the three shrill blows of a whistle tore us pitilessly from our exhausted sleep and from the longing of our dreams."
>
> Terrance de Pres, "Victory in the Concentration Camps," *Harper's Magazine,* Feb. 1992.

Where did those people get the strength to get up and go on? Some didn't, but many did. Walking in the valley of the shadow of death and loss can tear us pitilessly from the longing of our dreams. Where do we get the strength to go on? Where did Jesus' disciples get the strength to go on?

What made it possible for me, made it possible for you to go on, creatively, all those times. Notice I say what made it possible, not what made it easy. It is never easy. My answer, and I offer it to you for what it is worth, not out of any sense that I know all the answers, but in a certainty that I know what works for me. It is this: the God I have come to know, and have a relationship with, is congruent with the God Jesus told me about, and I trust that those whom I have lost in death will be all right with this God. This God,the God of Jesus, I trust. I bet my life on it. And that is no idle tale!

Believing that, having faith in this God, has allowed me to heal from losses, to return after grieving, to a creative expectancy and joy in this life. That is my testimony. After dozens of painful breaks in the family circle and countless other losses that were not death-related, which any of you could match, loss for loss, I came to understand that it is the nature of the God I have come to know through Jesus, who gives me the ability to grieve, and the hope to begin again. I think my experience parallels, at least in part, what the disciples experienced. They grieved the loss of Jesus. And they experienced him alive with them, not as a spook, not as a memory, not as a hallucination, but as a present person, and that for some extended period of time. Later, after Jesus was no longer present to them as a personal entity, they knew him as a present Holy Spirit.

Such confident hope in God and trust in the well-being of those lost to us is an exercise in faith. Hope is always a faith assumption, but it is not a wishful leap into empty space. Hope is an assumption that has roots. Christian hope is rooted in and always squares with what we trust about God and what we know about Christ, and what makes the most sense to us. This hope has always given me a usable future. And I am not alone in this faith.

> "If I were the only person who saw the sun rise this morning, then I might doubt my experience and call myself the victim of an illusion. But if I hear that many people in different countries and of varied intellectual powers have seen the same thing, and if I am told that men and women have laid down their lives rather than deny it, then my doubt vanishes; and I am sure of myself."
>
> Martin Camroux, "Is It True?" *Expository Times,* Nov. 1991, Page 53

I am not the only one to have seen the sun rise. I am not the only one to know and to give a resounding "yes" to the experience of knowing a God who can be trusted. I am not the only one to know the living Christ through the Holy Spirit, a spirit who has empowered me to trust God, to stand firm for the way of Jesus, to use whatever power I possess for the well-being of people Jesus points me to —the last and the least—and to trust that with God the dead are all right. I am not alone. Thus, by the power of God, I am confident that I can stand up in whatever chill happens in life and whatever darkness is to be faced. I can go on. I believe you can, too, faithfully and creatively.

...Then Hell Trembles

Daniel 14:23-27; Ephesians 6:10-20*

Rev. Dr. William C. Coleman

This sermon was preached at the Southern New England Conference, Springfield, Mass., June 9, 1990; at the United Methodist Church of Newton, Mass., Oct. 14, 1990; and at Calvary Church United Methodist, Arlington, Mass., Oct. 30, 1994.

*From the Vulgate, which includes Chapters 13 and 14 for Daniel; in most Protestant versions, Daniel ends after Chapter 12.

In C. S. Lewis' *Screwtape Letters* the devil in hell is giving advice to one of his agents on earth, assigned to keep a person from becoming an authentic Christian. The intended victim has joined the church and has the devil's agent worried. But Screwtape gives this assurance: "There is no need to despair ... if the victim does not see the church itself ... as we see her spread out through all time and space and rooted in eternity, terrible as an army with banners. That, I confess, is a spectacle which makes our boldest tempters uneasy." (page 15)

Lewis certainly presents a fanciful picture for us, doesn't he? But is there any truth to it? Does the authentic church, the company of faithful Christians—do these make hell tremble, to continue with Lewis' language for a moment? Or is this just metaphorical poetry? Imaginative religious fantasy? Wishful thinking?

When you think of the church with whom you worship regularly, pray with, plan with, work with, play with, celebrate the Lord's supper with, witness baptism and confirmation with ... is it a sight to make hell tremble? Or do you perceive it as a community, a people, a place which prompts demons to dance with glee? Those of us here with any sense of the church's local and world history know much about piety misguided. We know about the shameful deeds of injustice, pettiness, treachery, lechery, manipulation, persecution and bigoted crusades. We know about the caustic influences in the church of nationalism, racism, sexism, ageism and power plays that demand conformity based on cultural expectations that have nothing to do with any Gospel expectation or ethic— all done in the name of, and for the sake of, Jesus.

Now I admit there is a Catholic side of me that wants to overlook, to discount, to put aside these negatives. There is a side of me that doesn't want to face the dark side of the church's behavior; a side of me that wants to forget all that and to accent the positive. There is also a Protestant side of me that knows that the reformation of the church did not start in 1517, a side of me that knows that the reformation/Protestant principle began not long after Easter. Remember those fear-absorbed followers of Jesus? Then came Pentecost, wherein these fragile men and women were healed of their victim operating lifestyle. There is a side of me that knows from tradition and personal experience that the process of reformation and renewal is ever underway, though not always visible or necessarily steadily forward. But I am persuaded that reformation is always underway, under the initiative, guidance and hand of God. It is this remarkable capacity of God to bring about in the church, in us and in the world, renewal and transformation that makes hell tremble.

You ask about the nature of this hell? Let us leave the task to the systematic theologians and to the skilled philosophers to define hell, as to whether it is a place, a location, as many seem to imagine it to be. Personally I cannot truthfully say. Perhaps you and others can. Experientially, however, who of us cannot describe it as a *condition of being?* Despite loving surroundings there is a sense in which we live in hell. That is to say, we live in the midst of great psychic, socio-spiritual forces that impact and control much of what we call reality. As one person put it: "Sometimes I feel a hell in myself."

This self-hell can take at least two dimensions. One dimension is when one feels violated, abandoned, rejected, separated from others; the victim of horrible human forces or catastrophes, natural and human-made, that press us in on every side. This is the hell that others and events bring to us. The late Benjamin Mays, a black educator, mentor of Martin Luther King, and one of my favorite preachers, put it this way in describing the hell perpetrated on us by others and social forces:

> "All my life I have been uneasy about man. I recall as a boy how the people in my rural community in South Carolina used to go to a barbecue on Saturday or church on Sunday, drink, get drunk, shoot, and kill. I recall how I used to tremble in my bed in our house by the side of the road as drunken men late night, passed by, cursing, swearing, and shooting. At an early age I saw a mob ride, looking for a man to lynch."
>
> *Disturbed About Man,* Page 91.

There is a hell that others and events bring upon us!

Another dimension of hell is the misery we bring upon others, knowingly and unknowingly. It happens through the fostering of distrust by quasi-integrity to say nothing of our out-and-out dishonesty; our bent for revenge—getting even—as we say, our rapacious appetite for the world's goods and services far in excess of any legitimate need. We bring hell on others when our eye is forever on the bottom line, a prisoner of our own myopic notions of what is ultimately important—importance being defined as a profit at any cost, or winning at any cost, or believing that what we think is absolutely correct and good for everybody.

I have but modestly touched on the massive number of ways we can and do bring hell onto others. When we multiply our personal power with the power of the institutions of government, religion, finance, home, education, and so on, then we have an energy and authority that is awesome! If these are used as weapons to manage others into submission, then they become the power of hell. Ironically, we can do so with mindless innocence.

Editor James Wall, in an interview with Jimmy Carter, reported the former president's thinking about the changes and reformations that have taken place in his thinking and life over the past decade and a half.

> "I've been permitted a much wider range of observation in which I was able to grow out of a parochial experience, where

> you were sure you were right, where you know your particular religious interpretation is certain, and those who disagree with you are somehow inferior in the eyes of God ... as long as my only religious contacts were in the circle of friends in Plains (Georgia) and in the military, I didn't have to confront sincere people of a different (faith) viewpoint and listen with attention to their expression of different views."
>
> *Christian Century* , May 16, 1990, Page 515.

That is a prototype of the hell that we can bring on others, even when we think we're being religious, pious and faithful, when we are in fact being only ignorant, misinformed, and tragically foolish.

St. Paul understood this. In the morning New Testament text, he teaches us that in the Lord's power we can resist the devil's tactics. Now Paul is using the mythology, the worldview of his day, to talk about the reality of evil and the hell brought upon us and that we bring upon others. This worldview is wonderfully described in the Book of Daniel. There is a cosmic war between the God of creation and certain fallen angels. Especially potent, as they saw the matter, were Satan and his legions of demons who contend and struggle with God Almighty for loyalty of humankind's minds, hearts and lives. Paul uses code words for the evil forces in this divine struggle: he uses the common language of Daniel, "the principalities and the powers." And in this text Paul seems to say that it is with the principalities and the powers that we ultimately contend, and not with human enemies, as such.

Now what are we to make of all this? Some of you may hold the worldview of St. Paul—and in a fairly literal sense—and may find the mythology of St. Paul helpful and appropriate for you. So be it, if it assists you in allowing God to empower you toward more faithfulness to the truth of Christ. But let us be clear. There are other myths and worldviews held by people of faith, different from Paul's as they attempt to talk about this power of evil and hellish events and relationships. Some, who are influenced by modern psychology, may use a Freudian formula: the id, ego and super ego that can produce hellish conflicts. That perspective may be helpful, in that it speaks about working realities in human personality. But make no mistake, it is only a model, albeit a helpful one, in thinking about and understanding human behavior. But don't ever expect to see an "id, ego or super ego." And the fact is we all have our worldviews, our mythologies, our pictures by which we try to sort and organize reality.

Walter Wink, a biblical scholar, encourages us, however, not to lose the value of our biblical categories of principalities and the powers. Indeed, he says, it is important to recognize the major role played by the P's and P's in preventing God from acting as quickly to bring about renewal, reformation and liberation as we might like. Wink reminds us further as to the nature of these principalities and powers:

> "(They) are the massive institutions and social structures and systems that dominate our world today, and of the spirituality at their center. The 'powers' are not demonic beings floating in the sky; they are rather the (multi)national corporations, the nation states, the economic systems and the religious hierarchies that organize and, to a great extent, dictate the life of human societies."
>
> Vol. V, No. 2, *Weavings.*

These powers and principalities are not simply visible legal entities, but have inner spirit, an intangible, but discernible, corporate personality. These powers and principalities limit God, at least temporarily. In secular language we identify them by the phrase, "the powers that be." Yes, these powers limit God. The powers that be can and do assert their will against the will of God. Make no mistake about it and for a time, it may appear, they prevail over God.

How does this work? Some brief examples: God is creative and loving, gracious and kind, we believe. But if the principalities and the powers insist on being arms merchants to the world, all of which create jobs and gross national product, then as sure as night follows day the love of God, the graciousness of God, is hampered. In its stead will be hatred, violence and mayhem someplace where those armaments are used. God, we believe, is the God of truth who seeks to reveal the vast secrets of the world, the universe and beyond, and within our own hearts. But if the principalities and the powers insist on limiting truth-seeking and truth-telling by withholding financial support for education, or by intimidating those with a minority, unpopular viewpoint, and censoring teaching, then the truth revealing God is impeded. Ignorance, disease and hopelessness will then abound.

Or again, God is a liberator and seeks to bring the abundant life Jesus talked about to all humankind. We say, God has embedded in the soul, a love for liberty and freedom. But if the principalities and the powers insist on limiting people's access to sufficient food, meaningful work, choice of where to live, educational opportunities and with whom they will live and love through arbitrary things such as prohibitions based on race, gender, sexual orientation, nationality and class of origin, then God's capacity to develop people into their full potential is gravely obstructed.

Now you can rightly ask: "With God so limited, so impeded, so hampered, so obstructed, is God really God? At least in any meaningful sense of being God?" My answer is the answer of faith. Of course, God is God. But let us acknowledge that we simply do not know all the resources God brings to bear on the problems brought about by the principalities and the powers. I certainly do not know all the ways and means by which God almighty eventually overcomes the demonic side of the powers that be.

I do know well one resource, however. You and me. The church. Paul states it plainly: "We have to struggle against the darkness of this world." He goes on to give us a whole shopping list of resources to hold our ground—in Ephesians, the text read today. The military metaphor of military armor may not speak to where you live. It may be too grim for some of us. So let me try another from Daniel. I like the playfulness, the humor, the irony provided in Daniel. Now in most Protestant Bibles, Daniel ends after Chapter 12. A pity. The Jerusalem Bible, among others, includes two more chapters from the Vulgate Bible. In the 14th Chapter there is the delightful story of Daniel being faithful to God by feeding hairballs to a dragon that is being proposed as a suitable worship object. The dragon in his greed gobbles down the hairballs and subsequently bursts wide open, revealing a very mortal creature, one unworthy of worship and certainly inferior to the God of Jesus, the creator of life, to whom death is no threat. Feeding hairballs to dragons in the name of God—that makes hell tremble!

What hairballs shall we use? We have, of course, many suitable ones provided for us in the four Gospels, which Jesus teaches us. However, I want to choose only one, by way of illustration, to raise up for our reflection; one that is suggested by the Apostle Paul in Ephesians. All can do it. No one is excluded. It is *persistent prayer,* under the tutorage of Jesus. As Karl Barth once put it: "To close the hands in prayer is the beginning of an uprising against the demons and disorder of the world."

In the summer of 1989, Roz (my spouse) and I traveled in the USSR. While in Kishnev, the Moldavian capital, we visited the Cathedral Church. It had been closed as a church for 50 years, and only as recently as Feb. 1989 had been given back to the "believers" for restoration as the cathedral. When we were there in late June the walls were still bare, dusty, the building in a condition of being prepared for Christian use. The icons, rugs, Lord's table, candle racks, kneelers and more were still in crates, yet to be brought into the building's main sanctuary. However, that morning a lay woman was leading the daily office in the bare, main sanctuary. She was accompanied by perhaps 50 or so people of all ages. The service was recited in both Moldavian and Latin (they follow the Western rites). I thought, who knows how many prayers have been said in 50 years for just such a moment as this? The message came through clearly in the liturgy for the day: *"Christus Victor!"* Christ the Victor! At that very moment, I testify to you, I felt hell tremble!

Love in Living Deeds to Show

I John 4:16b-21

Rev. Dr. Robert Allen Moore

This sermon was preached at Niantic Community Church, Niantic, Conn., Sept. 14, 1997.

WHEN I WAS growing up, sex was never talked about at home. By the time I was in junior high, I knew everything there was to know about sex, of course. I knew, for example, that the worst thing I could call another boy was "queer" or "fag" or "fairy" or "homo." One time I went by myself to a movie theater in Boston, a man came and sat next to me. He put his hand on my knee. I remember the shock and perplexity I felt at that moment as I rushed from the theater. Why is a strange man doing this to me? Later, while I was working in the food service at Boston University, I made friends with several workers who were pleasant and gentle men. I later found out they were gay, and that was my first experience of realizing that a man could be gay and also be a decent person. These men were not sexual predators but people trying to come to grips with a realization that they were different from heterosexual men.

Around the same time, two of my male friends in theological school announced that they were going to be married. This announcement sent shock waves through the school. A United Methodist pastor in Boston officiated at their service and for doing so was forced into early retirement and thus out of active United Methodist ministry. I remember being impressed with the courage of his convictions. When I was in my 20s, one of my cousins married a pediatrician. He was kind, gentle, smart, compassionate, and fun to be with. He and my cousin had two children.

After they had been married for 10 or 20 years, he recognized that he was gay. This event created an enormous stir in our entire family, but we continued to love and accept him because we knew what a wonderful man he was.

These events influenced my thinking about homosexuality. I began to realize that the myths and stereotypes I had learned growing up needed to be examined. I learned that so many people who have contributed so much to human history were gay or lesbian. It is an impressive list that includes the following: Socrates, Aristotle, Leonardo da Vinci, Michelangelo, John Milton, Hans Christian Andersen, John Maynard Keynes, Lawrence of Arabia, Walt Whitman, Bessie Smith, Peter Illyich Tlachaikowski, Virginia Woolf, Gertrude Stein, Rudolf Nereyev, May Sarton, W. H. Auden, Willa Cather, Horatio Alger, Benjamin Britten, Adrienne Rich, Leonard Bernstein, Dag Hammersjold. The list goes on, of course, and includes people who have made enormous contributions to government, economics, the arts, and sciences.

So what, you ask? Why does this belong in a sermon in church? Here are two reasons. 1.) No issue has so divided the church since the days of slavery, not even the abortion issue. If an issue is this big in the church, it is probably important for us to spend some time with it. 2.) We face a fundamental theological question here. If God created us in the divine image, did God create some people gay and lesbian or is that something they chose?

Let me say a few things in response to that second question. Are people homosexual by choice or is it something that is given as part of their basic identity? That is, did God make them that way or did they choose to be that way? I don't know. Science doesn't know, but growing evidence from science suggests that it is a given. Perhaps the best thing we have to go by is the testimony of gays and lesbians who know deep in their souls that their sexual identity has been given, not chosen. Is that a reliable basis for answering the question? I don't know, but I have to wonder why anyone, given the hostility that gays and lesbians face in their lives, would choose to be that way. Over and over, the testimony we hear from gays and lesbians is "God made us this way." But some would say, "God did not make them that way. God made us male and female to propagate the species. Homosexuality is unnatural, a sin against nature." Is it? I don't know, but I have to ask whether God created people with the ability to love and to be intimate only for the purpose of procreation? Is it possible that God is just as interested in two people, whether of the same or different sexes, finding joy and fulfillment in a faithful, self-giving monogamous relationship?

Maybe you believe that gays and lesbians are perverts. If we take a look at where we see perversion, it will be much easier to find it among heterosexuals. Witness the raunchy heterosexual displays on TV, in movies and in our culture. Yes, we see bizarre behavior among gays and lesbians, but they are not representative of the homosexual population as a whole. We live in an age of excess; some people both gay and straight will push the boundaries of acceptable behavior to the limit. But as I observe it, this is much more a straight than a gay phenomenon. It is worth noting that most rapists and pedophiles are heterosexual. Are gays and lesbians perverts? I don't know, but by and large there seems to be little if any evidence to support that claim.

Perhaps you will say: "The Bible certainly condemns homosexuality. How can you, as a minister of the Gospel, suggest that a gay and lesbian lifestyle might be OK?" I'm going to touch on this only very briefly, because you will have the chance on the next four Wednesday nights to study closely and carefully what the Bible says on this subject. It is true that the Bible says some terrible things about homosexuals. But the Bible says equally bad things about adultery and swearing at your parents and eating shellfish. Leviticus proposed some severe punishments for such things. Interestingly we don't take those things very seriously. As you should not. So why would we take literally as a divine decree the injunction from Leviticus which says that same sex people who engage in sexual intimacy shall be put to death? Of course, we shouldn't take the prohibition and the proposed punishment as literally applicable to us today. But if we did take Leviticus literally, we would also be obliged to condemn equally almost everyone sitting here today. When it comes to interpreting Scripture, all of us - including the literalists and fundamentalists—become selective fundamentalists. As Bill Coffin puts it in his typically insightful way, "Too many Christians use the Bible as a drunk uses a lamppost - for support rather than illumination." He goes on to write in his book *A Passion for the Possible:*

> "Clearly it is not Scripture that creates hostility to homosexuality, rather hostility to homosexuality that prompts some Christians to recite a few sentences from Paul and random passages from an otherwise discarded Old Testament code. In abolishing slavery and in ordaining women, we've gone beyond literalism. It's time we did the same with gays and lesbians. The problem is not how to reconcile homosexuality with scriptural passages that condemn it, but rather how to reconcile the rejection and punishment of homosexuals with the love of Christ. It can't be done. So instead of harping on what's 'natural,' let's talk of what's 'normal,' what operates according to the norm. For Christians the norm is Christ's love. If people can show the tenderness and constancy in caring that honors Christ's love, what matters their sexual orientation? Shouldn't a relationship be judged by its inner worth rather than its outer appearance? When has a monopoly on a durable life- warming love been held by legally wed heterosexuals?"

There is one last comment to make about the Bible and homosexuality: What did Jesus say about homosexuality? Nothing. Absolutely nothing. Now you would think that if this were so important a subject, Jesus would have had something to say about it. As I said earlier, I don't claim to know the whole truth about the subject, but the Bible tells me that God is a God of love, not condemnation and my heart tells me that, in this age of throw-away relationships, God rejoices when faithful love exists between two caring people, whether gay or straight.

It is love that must stand as the guiding principle for our living. For as we read in I John 4:18, *"There is no fear in love, but perfect love casts out fear."* Love is what banishes fear and prejudice, what allows us to grow in understanding, freedom and compassion. It was love that made Jesus draw to himself those whom the world abandoned. How can we who live in his love and walk in his way do anything less?

Wings Like Eagles

Isaiah 40:28-31

Rev. Dr. Robert Alan Moore

This sermon was preached at Niantic Community Church, Niantic, Conn., Feb. 6, 2000.

THE YEAR HAS gotten off to a very bad start for me, so this text is definitely good news to me this morning. I was sick for a week with an upper respiratory affliction. Then I felt good for a week until it came back on me twice as bad as the first time. Just as I was about recovered from that, I slipped on the ice and broke a rib. Have you ever broken a rib? Don't. It's the most painful injury I've ever had. I am a bit better now, but I'm still not running. In fact I'm hardly walking yet. At least I haven't fainted. But in the overall scale of things, this is small stuff.

Have you ever had a sense of weariness that overwhelmed you? Maybe it has to do with health problems or financial problems, or marriage problems, or parental problems. Any of those alone is hard enough, but when they bunch up, we can find ourselves feeling discouraged, defeated and depressed.

That's exactly how the people of Israel felt at the time this word of hope was written. Israel has been defeated by its surrounding nations, its leading citizens deported to Babylon where they live in exile. Looking back on their history, Isaiah announces that their exile is God's punishment for their sins. The prophet names those sins very explicitly. Now, however, the prophet announces that the time of exile is over. Those who have found themselves feeling discouraged, defeated and depressed are told that their sins are forgiven and that they will be given new strength to return home and rebuild their lives.

The good news Isaiah announces is that in God there is new life and strength to meet discouragement, defeat and depression. It is more than Garrison Keillor's Powder Milk Biscuits from Lake Wobegone that give shy people the strength to get up and do what needs to be done. God gives life and strength to face and overcome the worst that life can deal us.

Some people seem to be immune to discouragement, defeat and depression; they can just keep chugging along like the EverReady Bunny. John Wesley was told by a certain Mr. Henry in 1785: "I bless God that I am never tired *of* my work, yet I am often tired in my work."

> Wesley replied: "By the blessing of God, I can say more: I am never tired in my work. From the beginning of the day or the week or the year to the end I do not know what weariness means. I am never weary of writing or preaching or traveling; but I am just as fresh at the end as at the beginning. Thus it is with me today, and I take no thought of tomorrow."

I've known people like that. I get tired just hearing them talk of all they're doing. Some people can go on and on like that until they die and are at peace—and so are we. But most of us grow weary or grow discouraged or grow disconsolate. Like the people in exile in Babylon.

Maybe one of the secrets of life is to honestly acknowledge that negative side of life, to recognize that there are times when we feel that we are in exile, but not to get stuck in it. And also to avoid getting stuck in a Pollyanna state where we deny the negative side of life by adopting a false view that this is the best of all possible worlds. My favorite novel is Herman Melville's *Moby Dick.* If I had to live with one passage that distills Melville's wisdom for me, it would be a certain passage from Chapter 96, "The Try-Works." Ismael, the narrator, has fallen asleep at the helm while gazing into the fire of the try-works, the huge cauldron in which the whale blubber is boiled down to extract its oil for putting in barrels and bringing back to sell. He catches himself just in time to prevent the ship from capsizing and then launches into one of those wonderful Melvillean soliloquies:

> "Look not too long in the face of the fire, O man! Never dream with thy hand on the helm! Turn not thy back to the

compass; accept the first hint of the hitching tiller; believe not the artificial fire when its redness makes all things look ghastly. To-morrow, in the natural sun, the skies will be bright; those who glared like devils in the forking flames, the morn will show in far other, at least gentler, relief: the glorious, golden, glad sun, the only true lamp-all others but liars!

Nevertheless the sun hides not Virginia's Dismal Swamp, nor Rome's accursed Campagna, nor the wide Sahara nor all the millions of miles of deserts and of griefs beneath the moon. The sun hides not the ocean, which is the dark side of the earth, and which is two-thirds of the earth. So, therefore, that mortal man who hath more of joy than sorrow in him, that mortal man cannot be true—not true, or undeveloped. With books the same. The truest of all men was the Man of Sorrows, and the truest of all books is Solomon's, and Ecclesiastes is the hammered steel of woe. All is vanity. ALL. This willful world hath not got hold of unchristian Solomon's wisdom yet.

But even Solomon, he says, 'the man that wandereth out of the way of understanding shall remain (i.e. even while living) in the congregation of the dead.' Give not thyself up, then, to fire, lest it invert thee, deaden thee, as for the time it did me. There is a wisdom that is woe, but there is a woe that is madness. And there is a Catskill eagle in some souls that can alike dive down into the blackest gorges and soar out of them again and become invisible in the sunny spaces. And even if he forever flies within the gorge, that gorge is in the mountains; so that even in his lowest swoop the mountain eagle is still higher than other birds upon the plain, even though they soar."

May we be people of faith who can look squarely at the world's woe and neither be overwhelmed by it nor be blind to the way it calls out to us for our response. May we mount up with wings like a Catskill eagle, that our spirits may soar, even if we be in the darkest gorges of life.

As we draw near to the Lord in this holy meal today, may we who wait upon the Lord receive from the Lord the strength to mount up with wings like eagles, remembering, in the words of one of the first communion hymns of the Christian Church:

> Here, O my Lord, I see thee face to face;
> Here would I touch and handle things unseen;
> Here grasp with firmer hand eternal grace,
> And all my weariness upon thee lean.

— The United Methodist Hymnal,
The UnitedMethodist Publishing House, 1989, p.623.

Today Is Easter

John 20:1-18

Rev. Dr. Mark A. Fowler

This sermon was preached at Carter Memorial United Methodist Church, Needham, Mass., March 30, 1997.

Introduction

THE WOMEN RAN to tell the disciples that they had seen the risen Lord! Early on the first day of the week the disciples were filled with Good Friday fear instilled by the horrible crucifixion of Jesus on the Hill of the Skull; they were frightened in their beds when the women arrived with the news:

"He is Risen!"

I met one of these women as she was grinding corn into meal for tortillas. We were in the mountains of the border region between Honduras and Nicaragua. We had been up all night in the neighborhood home that was scheduled to keep the vigil. We were to give the alarm to the *barrio* if the soldiers came. In the morning we went out to check to see if everyone was all right. The door to a one-room home was open to let the morning breeze blow through. A woman was alone and she was obviously pregnant. In the corner of the room a small table had been set up as an altar. There were honored pictures of two children and a man. The soldiers had killed one of the children along with her teacher and the rest of the class simply because they were learning to read. Several months later the second child was killed by the soldiers early one morning while picking coffee. I stood staring at the pictures of lives snuffed out and now only cherished in this home on this altar and in the altar of their mother's heart. A heart that was burdened with grief.

She had become pregnant shortly after the death of her second child. And then, her husband had been killed in a raid on the village. "How can you possibly bear having another child?" I asked. "Nothing has changed, the soldiers still surround you, they might ..." She knew the risks and dangers. She put a hand over the cross around her neck and another gently caressed the child she was carrying. "If I don't, then death wins. They win. Jesus came back to life to give us hope. Without this, there is no hope and no reason to live."

She is one of the women who has spoken to my disciple's fear and testified to the truth of the risen Christ! Praise God who has given us the victory of life through our Lord Jesus Christ. Through the risen Christ, we are born anew to a living hope and an abundant life which is not temporary or bound by the threat of death, but is eternal and must be embraced in its fullness.

One

Today is Easter Day! Today is the day when we claim the eternal victory of life over death!

Today is Easter Day! Today is the day when we claim the eternal victory of hope over despair!

Today is Easter Day! Today is the day when we claim the eternal victory of peace over the horrors of war, poverty, racism, prejudice, hatred and strife!

Today is Easter Day! Today is the day when we claim the eternal victory of human dignity and stand together as the children of God in our rightful places as those who are a little lower than the angels.

Today is Easter Day! Today is the day when our sins and brokenness are wiped away and the new day dawns and the future begins, washed in the waters of salvation. Filled with the breath of God, the spark of life itself. It is the same Holy Spirit who has raised Jesus Christ from the dead and has been the instrument of our calling and formed us into a living body to continue the work of redemption. And to continue the work of hope so that the abundance of life on this earth would flourish. That is the hope of

God for creation and the assurance of God at the resurrection! God loved the world so much that God gave the only begotten son, that whosoever believes in him should not perish, but have everlasting life!

Today is Easter! Today is the day when the goodness of creation and the worth of your life is affirmed and claimed by the eternal love of God which comes to you in the risen Lord!

Two

I say these things as a witness to the resurrection in the same week as 39 of God's children took their own lives in a mansion in California. A tragic horror. The adherents of Heaven's Gate held a twisted and dangerous faith which mixed in a philosophy of neo-Platonism, which teaches that the spirit realm, above and beyond this earth, is far better than our mortal experience. Spirit and body are torn apart, separated from each other. When they are combined they live uncomfortably together. The creation is despised so much that the greatest gift which God has bestowed, the gift of life itself, is thrown away in the tragic belief that it is not worth living. Mix that philosophy with a false understanding of the resurrection as a spiritual release from creation and the result is the tragedy of Rancho Santa Fe.

My sisters and my brothers, we must stand firm in the light of the resurrection and hold to the truth that the victory of Easter is the victory of life over death. Life here. Life now. The faith of the church has always been the physical resurrection of Jesus Christ from the dead. And, on this particular Easter I have come to understand the imperatives of that particular aspect of the Christian faith. The physical resurrection of Christ is to bless the eternal worth and nature of life itself. Jesus Christ rose from the dead, a physical body, as the victory of life over death. In his resurrection Jesus formed us into that physical body, the church, to carry on his ministry of blessing life itself and to nurture it in all of its abundance. Christ opened the door to heaven to assure us of where we are going in the great beyond. That was so that we could give our whole faith and our whole energy and our whole life to the blessing of this life. Here and now!

Listen! He blessed on that mountainside by the Sea of Galilee for the abundance of life.

Listen! He healed the sick and restored life to Jarus' daughter and Lazarus for the abundance of this life.

Listen! He struggled against the confining and spirit crushing rules of religion to liberate the spirit of life in each of us for the living of these days.

Listen! He condemned oppression and poverty and lifted up the broken hearted for the living of this life.

Listen! He made it simple! Love the Lord your God with all of your heart, mind, soul and strength ... and love your neighbor as yourself. For the living of this life.

Three

Jesus came in his physical resurrection to begin the fulfillment of the prayer he had taught his disciples, "Thy will be done on earth as it is in heaven." The dwelling of God is with humankind.

About a year ago, a blessed member of our church was very ill with thyroid cancer. Tom Markert had battled it bravely, with faith and hope that he would be cured. But, greater than his faith in a cure was his embrace of life. Even as his body diminished he continued to live and live fully. The love he shared with his wife, Angie, deepened in extraordinary ways. Love God and love your closest neighbor. Those of us who visited Tom could not see him as a man who was dying, but a man who was eternally alive.

I remember when some of you asked me how long Tom had to live. The question seemed to me to be reasonable, yet absurd in the face of the Tom I encountered when I saw him. *Tom had the rest of his life to live!* Each day was lived as a victory for life. Each hour was an opportunity to live the eternal reality of Christ. Each moment was an opportunity to love God and reach out and touch his neighbor. Even in the last hours of his life he was planning mission work on behalf of the risen Lord. Even in the middle of the night, when his body was so weak he could hardly move, he would use what energy he had to ring for the nurses that Angie would be covered with a blanket and gave instruction that it be done with care not to wake her. He didn't want her to chill in the cool of the night. *Tom knew the risen Lord! Tom had faith in the blessings of his life! Tom knew where he was going, that Christ has opened heaven to him! So he had the rest of his life to live! Abundantly!*

Today, Tom is with the Lord in heaven, as the Lord was with Tom in the abundance of the Easter life here with us.

Conclusion

My sisters and my brothers, in a world that is filled with difficulty, evil, stress, loneliness, vanity, arrogance and horror ... all of which conspired to take the life of our savior in the agonizing death on Calvary's hills ... he has risen and vanquished the power of them all. Life, the abundant life which God has blessed for us will flourish. Join with the woman who found hope in the life of a baby to be born, despite what a frightened disciple has said to her. Join Tom and live the rest of your life extravagantly loving your neighbor and boundlessly loving your God despite the questions and realities which may nag us with the limits of life. For he is risen and has won for us the victory of life. He is risen indeed!

Restored to Life

Ezekiel 37:1-14; John 11:1-45

Rev. Dr. Mark A. Fowler

This sermon was preached at Boston University Marsh Chapel, Boston, Mass., March 19, 1996.

Introduction

"And Jesus stepped to the mouth of the tomb and called into the dark abyss, "Lazarus, come out and live."

THE TEMPERATURES HAVE been playing a Lenten game with us lately. One day they will tempt us to believe that spring has come. The milling students on Commonwealth Ave. will respond with shorts and tank tops. And, the next day's sky will gray with snow or frigid rain. The chill of wintry death plays with the life-birthing hope of spring.

One evening I was disturbed in my sleep by the constant rush of a driving rain. The force of wind was unmerciful to the trees which surround my home, bending their sinew to the breaking point, the macabre shadows playing on the wall of my bedroom. The rain cascaded across the driveway and matted the brown grass. The windows rattled in the wind and the flagpole chattered in its stand. How strangely disturbing this all was. So much activity, but little life in the middle of the night.

I walked through the house, lit only by streetlights and lawn lanterns whose beams wavered in the wind. A gleam caught a dusty and unused vase that had waited through the winter for the flowers that would fill it later in the spring. It sat on a bare table whose holiday cloth had been removed after Christmas. Another, with bright prints would not return until the weather was better and guests invited.

I opened the door to fasten a loose shutter. The wood chips and mulches were blowing out of the barren flowerbeds and spreading on the lawn. The skeletal fingers of the bushes scratched at the empty air. I knew that beneath was life waiting to burst forth in beautiful color, and that soft breezes and gentle rains would caress it. But, that was below this violent and hostile exterior of reality.

This was the last Lenten gasp of a prolonged winter of storms before the daffodils, lilies and butterflies emerging from their chrysalis would herald the resurrection of Easter. "*Lenzin,*" our German ancestors used to call it. A time when the altar is decorated with the colors of the deepest sea and the pastors are wrapped in the mollusk's purple. A time when all things seem to pass through a natural depression brought on by the seclusion of a lengthening winter.

Standing on the porch, I am aware that this storm will pass soon. I have heard a lone bird calling to its mate to return home. Spring is coming. The wind pierces my skin with the stinging rain. The storm is not quite over; Easter is not yet here. There is still no life in the flowerbeds. There is brown grass, an empty vase, a barren dining table.

One

Jesus went to the mouth of the tomb where the dead Lazarus lay. The endless, hollow abyss yawned before him. The air was thick with death. And, Jesus called forth life!

The March winds blow into the hollow and dead places of our souls, of our experiences, of our communities, of our pale hopes. The Lenten winds of prayer, fasting and self-examination expose them, just as Lazarus' tomb was exposed when they rolled the stone away. The exposure of our souls in Lent is a struggle ... remember the great protest of the villagers in Bethany when Jesus asked them to expose the tomb of Lazarus. "NOOO! There will be a stench!" Precisely! This is the time to expose the stench. And, to trust that it is into that stinking abyss that Jesus steps and calls forth a new and abundant life.

Two

We live in times of rapid change and mobility. It brings with it a great sense of personal displacement and alienation. We all become strangers in a strange land. What is familiar and fulfilling is often replaced by what is strange and it evokes feelings of emptiness, of being only partial, perhaps even abysmal.

When I was 18, I left my home in the city of Lynn on the North Shore to attend a good Methodist College, De Pauw University, in Greencastle, Indiana. As many of you probably have noticed in your sojourn here in Boston, those of us who grew up in this area believe that the world ends at Route 128, perhaps stretching to Route 495 these days. Positively wilderness beyond those landmarks. I had enrolled at De Pauw sight unseen. My family didn't have the money for that summer-after-junior-year-in-high-school college visitation trip. I saw it only in the catalog!

The night before our arrival at De Pauw we stayed in Indianapolis, a *city*! If that is what Greencastle is going to be like, I thought I could survive. But, I was sorely mistaken. Next morning, we headed west, past the city limits which turn almost immediately into farm country!

I was scared to death! Bales of rolled hay. Cornfields. Buildings with acres between them. I leaned over and asked my father, a De Pauw alum, "What do people do out here?" He simply laughed. I prayed, "God, please take me home." The closer we got to De Pauw, the simpler the prayer, "At least make this place big enough for a traffic light. All I've seen is stop signs."

Without great buildings and traffic patterns and the urban environment, I had trouble getting my bearings, trouble figuring out who I was or what I was supposed to do. In a real way, much of what had defined who I was had died. No one knew me. Nothing was familiar. The marking stones I had depended on had gone.

In parish ministry I have learned that those difficult transitions mark a great deal of what we do. Grief at the loss of a loved one, saying "hello" to a new family and "goodbye" to a cherished one. Dealing with the loss of employment. Helping families cope with the traumatic and dramatic changes which occur within it. These are the times of movement and change when the familiar vanishes or is transformed in unrecognizable ways.

And, in the middle of my time in college, when I was just getting my feet oriented in a career path toward the theater, God came into my life and called me into the ordained ministry. As a senior in college I was appointed as a local pastor to the United Methodist Church in Putnamville, Indiana. Population 102. Eighty-five of them were Methodists. At the first hymn sing, they asked if I would pick out some of the old favorites. I picked out some of my favorites, but it seemed as if they were a bit reserved in their singing. All right, I was actually singing a solo. So I asked them to tell me one of their favorites. In unison they called for "Little Church in the Wildwood." I had never heard of it! But, I sang along, "There is nothing so dear to my childhood as the little brown church in the vale. ..." The lay leader sidled up to me and said, "Doesn't that just warm your heart?" Truth to tell, it didn't. Dear to my childhood was a tall steepled church surrounded by triple-decker tenements.

In my remembrance, ministry had to do with meeting parishioners at their offices and businesses or climbing apartment steps; not walking corn rows and sitting at the only coffee shop in town which doubled as the post office, police station and fire dispatcher. In those years, years that began with loneliness, emptiness, confusion, and a feeling of being alien and lost, wanting to go home, God stepped into those places and called forth new life. A life that now cherished the church in the wildwood.

When I graduated from the School of Theology (Boston University), one of my classmates returned to the Minnesota Conference. She was raised in Minneapolis and loved the city (she thrived here in Boston). The bishop appointed her to Pipestone. To get there you went hundreds of miles from anywhere, turned right and kept going. Pipestone is a crossroad. She was miserable. It was the end of the summer and she wondered what she should to do feel better. I suggested that she go visiting. She said there wouldn't be anyone home; they were all out harvesting. I suggested that she get her boots on and walk the fields with them. "I don't wear boots!" she said. "I don't want to wear boots!"

Hear her? I don't want to roll the stone away. ... I don't want to like it here. ... I really don't want to pastor these people. ... I want to go home to Minneapolis and pastor there.

Three

During my first year at the School of Theology I was appointed to serve the Boston Street United Methodist Church in Lynn. My old stomping grounds, but on the rival side of the city. The first Sunday I was to preach was the first Sunday after Christmas. I had seen the sanctuary. It could hold 600 people in richly padded mahogany pews. A huge organ graced the choir loft, with three manuals and more stops that I could count. Forty seats for choir members surrounded the organ. Quite a large step from Putnamville.

On that Sunday I arrived half an hour before the service. I came to the choir to pray with them. There were four. I hoped the rest would come later. There were no more. I went into the sanctuary and sat in the big chair behind the large pulpit and prayed. It was a vast pulpit that blocked my view of the sanctuary. After praying, I peeked around the pulpit and saw 25 people being swallowed by that gargantuan hall. Most of them were in their last years of work. Actually, most of them were in their last years. I remembered Harrell Beck used to remind us of appointments like this in Hebrew Bible classes. When teaching Ezekiel he said that there would a moment when you would hear the Lord ask from behind the reredos, "Can these bones live?" That is when a young pastor takes the leap of faith and replies, "Lord, thou knowest!"

Boston Street Church had, at one time, been a great church in the city of Lynn, which had at one time been the center of Methodism in New England. It had numbered 14 United Methodist churches within the city limits. I had been sent to Boston Street Church to close it. Eight other United Methodist churches had already been closed in the city. Demographics had changed. The economy had turned sour, personalities had clashed, and people's interest had turned to other things. Boston Street Church was going to join the others in heading toward closure and sure death. It would dissolve and never be heard from again.

In our own lives things change beyond our control: We lose a job. Our gifts do not carry us as far as we want to go. Our sight fails. We go deaf. Relationships are damaged seemingly beyond repair. The life of our church is disrupted and threatened. Lazarus gets sick and dies. We are hurt and empty, hollow. We experience alienation or even death.

It is precisely in these situations that God dedicated the greatest amount of life energy. Lazarus is dead. Martha was consumed by her anger and Mary was disabled by her grief. And, Jesus stepped to the mouth of the abyss and called forth life: "Unbind Lazarus from the grave clothes and let him live!" His call not only revived Lazarus, but also energized Mary to celebration and harnessed Martha's anger to mission zeal.

It was in the waning years of the Boston Street Church, when it carried a death sentence in its body, that Jesus stood at the abyss of the future of that church and called it to life. In those years, the members of that church heard the call of Christ to evangelism and doubled the membership. But not just to keep the doors open; rather to be in mission in the city. In those waning years, the membership of that church began new mission projects in the city and put together a foundation which would fund mission outreach to youth of the city, the homeless and senior citizens. Their vision of ministry was far beyond the existence of the building or even the life span of the faithful community. You see, they were already in the tomb when I met them. They were Lazarus. Yet, the last three years of their experience as a church was in listening to Christ calling into their abyss and leading them to a new life, a new purpose and a new hope. It was uncomfortable. In fact, at times it was downright painful to lose what was familiar and cherished and to move out in faith to where Christ was leading.

Conclusion

The howling of the wind had pierced the hollows of my soul out there on the porch. The darkness of the night had put me in my place, reminding me that I was not sure what the future held. I was not sure what hollows and pains I would sustain and how Christ would invite me to come out of them. But, I have heard Jesus call Lazarus to come out and live, to be unbound and free to follow the Lord, to live in the faith of Christ's call to new life.

My Prayers ... and the Other Children

Genesis 1:26-31; Matthew 7:7-12

Rev. David A. Hollenbeck

This sermon was preached at the New England Annual Conference, June 1993 and at Calvary Church United Methodist, Arlington, Mass., Jan. 17, 1999.

MY SON, LEE, was hit by a truck when he was five years old so this particular story jumped at me from the pages of the *Christian Century* magazine. It is from a meditation by the Rev. Suzanne Guthrie. It is the story of a little boy calling home for a ride after his music lesson.

"Come on Mom, it's hot and I'm tired. It's a long way home."

"Oh, Jack, you've walked it many times and I'm really busy."

Mother reluctantly goes to pick him up and when she arrives there is a horror scene. A young man has just struck another child with his sports car and there is chaos ... an ambulance ... crying ... a single shoe lying in the crosswalk.

"Jack, do you know the boy?"

"No Mom, but I can't look at him."

They get into their car.

"Oh, Jack, pray as hard as you can."

They go home and times passes, but Mom can't get the scene out of her mind. She reflects: "I cannot merely be thankful that the tragedy did not happen to me. Prayer breaks down the illusion of separation between the victim, the unwilling agent of evil, and those of us who believe we are watching from the outer circle of spectators."

> "I am in the mother at the hospital."
> "I am the boy lying unconscious."
> "I am in the young man racing his car to pick up
> a tuxedo to look nice for his date tonight."

And then she says:

> "We are all one in some obscure way
> that we will never understand until
> we truly learn to love.
> Perhaps ... if I prayed for the world with
> the same ardor I pray for my own children,
> I could understand this better."

The New Testament lesson includes one of the best-known verses in the Bible. We call it the Golden Rule: "Do unto others as you would have them do to you." Some of the commentaries say: This is the law and the Prophets in a nutshell. Keep this and you will be keeping all the other rules. Jesus is saying, "What you wish for your treatment, do unto others." Our temptation is to oversimplify these words and forget how directly they are related to the major heartaches of the world. And, to forget how directly they are connected time and time again to discrimination based on the color of skin.

A significant portion of the violence that comes into our living rooms on what we sadly and casually call "news" is a direct result of a seemingly endless line of discrimination. This is a problem that includes and involves every one of us, and our churches will not be part of the solution with just a reluctant collection on Race Relations Sunday, a pensive remembrance of 30 years since Robert Kennedy's death, or the use of a bulletin with a nice picture near the birthday of Martin Luther King Jr.

I believe that what we are talking about is more than an issue of civil rights, race relations, or even discrimination. It is more than a social dilemma. It is a matter of not understanding creation itself and who God intended we would be and what we would do ... with the gift ... the gift of life itself! How we see and think about people who are different than we are in any way, is part of our everyday lives and the reactions are very subtle. Most of us are not aware of it when we go about teaching discrimination. This story is from the book entitled *The Black Child,* by Phyllis Harrison Ross and Barbara Wyden. Charlie was 5 months old, blue-eyed and blond. His mother had just taken him to the pediatrician for his shots and when finished, got on the elevator to come down to the ground floor. A black man also got on. Mother began to think about the items on the news and the things she had heard. She held Charlie a little tighter and he began to whimper. Charlie noticed a different look on his mother's face. She told him he had been a good boy for his shots, but she held him tighter and they both felt uneasy. The elevator arrived on ground floor and they went their separate ways. She didn't think about it anymore. But she should have, for she had just given Charlie his first lesson in bigotry.

We take great pains to teach the children in our homes the correct manners: "Please" and "thank you" are still the magic words. Safety is also taught: "Don't play with matches," "Watch and look and listen when you cross the street." We teach sharing and responsibility: "Please pick up your toys and hang up your clothes." I believe we also have a responsibility to teach that differences are a natural part of God's world and that people just like us are not better in any way than people who are different from us. The Golden Rule is not just pertaining to those who look and act like us ... it means we treat all others as we want to be treated. I believe that acceptance of differences as a good and natural part of God's creation can be taught in our homes, schools, neighborhoods and churches. And, if we don't do it now, it is not too late to begin. It is a wonderful thing for a child to hear a parent say, "You know, I think I have been wrong," and then see the parent act, think and speak differently. A church can do this too!

It's hard to change because many people around us want us to behave as we always have. If we stop making fun of American Indians, if we stop laughing at ethnic jokes and begin to voice different attitudes about people of all colors, our friends may be uncomfortable, but it is not too late for any of us to make changes. All of us can make a point to say positive instead of negative things. We have parents tell us that in Sunday school they want their children to learn certain time-honored things as well as a philosophy of life. They want them to learn the Ten Commandments, the 23rd Psalm, the Lord's Prayer. Learning to treat others as we would like to be treated is also something we need to learn and relearn, teach and teach again and again ... throughout our lives.

I believe that we should have a worldview that does not put other people down. I don't think any one group, nationality, religion, or race has all the truth. Keep in mind that the person who drove the Jeep full of dynamite into the barracks in Lebanon a few years ago and killed 280 sleeping black and white U.S. Marines was a very religious person. He simply believed that his point of view was the only right one and therefore nothing else and no one else mattered.

When we become increasingly narrow ... when religious selfishness of any faith shrinks our minds and hearts so that the view from our eyes is squeezed so small that there is not even room for a Golden Rule, we have lost touch with the idea of being created in God's image. When our rigid hardness of heart drives the socially wounded to Waco, or to Montana (sites of violent deaths in struggles between citizens and government officials), or to millennium madness ... when our greed makes us constantly think up new reasons to justify and rationalize our maintenance of an underclass because it makes life easier for us ... when we are unwilling to examine our own beliefs and behaviors, then we are part of the problem!

We have made excuses for generations to justify inhuman treatment of God's children on every continent and in every country. And, a crucial factor has always been the color of skin and our own inability to feel comfortable and not threatened by people who are different in some way than we are. The Golden Rule takes on another dimension, doesn't it, when we insert the issue of skin color? Do unto others of every color, of every nationality, of every language, of every sexual orientation—all others—male and female, as you would have them do unto you.

I believe that the goal is not to pretend that there are no differences in people. Even very young children notice that there are many differences in people. The goal is to believe and teach that differences

... are not important,
... are not negative,
... and most important of all, they (differences) are the way
God created us, "and saw that it was very good." The violet

and the orchid are very different and both very beautiful.

When we mention the Golden Rule we may think of something for small children in Sunday school to learn at an early age, because the Golden Rule is easy. Right? Wrong! I hear American tourists in other countries be angry, irritated with the native population who do not speak English—to make tourist stays easier. And we who are the children and grandchildren of immigrants look at those who want now to enter our country, and we may think and say: "They want our money, our health and our education." We look at them and think, "Why don't they stay where they are and do better right there?" The moment that finances in a town, country, world, church or family begin to crumble, everyone starts to blame someone else, and "scapegoating" begins. Hate crimes increase, people begin persecutions for ethnic, racial and religious reasons. We listen to the voices of the David Dukes or some other bigoted personality, who coat evil actions and attitudes with false labels of family values, Christian beliefs ... phrases which delude the mind and kill the soul ... things that sound good but are a lie at the same time.

My friends, we have a unique opportunity in our churches to do something that makes a difference. We have people of all ages: babies, children, youth, adults in every decade of life coming to us and saying,

> ... teach us about life;
> ... tell us how God wants us to think and live;
> ... tell us how to benefit from our mistakes so that
> the future will be better for us and for our children and their children;
> ... instruct us how to accept God's forgiveness, and to
> understand all the hurt, and to use the teachings of Jesus to
> make our lives more like they ought to be. We want the
> world to be a better place. Can we help?;
> ... how can we change so that we can recognize ourselves as
> created in God's image?;
> ... and will you love us? Will you love us? Love us enough to
> do any of these things we ask? Enough to be part of acting
> out the reality of God's creation and re-creation?

Each week we are collectively part of churches where thousands of people come asking, looking, listening and seeking. Part of their answer comes when each one of us listens and hears the word:

> ... from the story of creation to the Golden Rule,
> ... from the birth in Bethlehem to the empty tomb.

How we hear that word, and what we do, and how we act is a crucial factor in the answer they find!

Now, let's flash back to that mother and her healthy unharmed child who has called her to pick him up after his music lesson—the dented sports car—the single shoe lying in the crosswalk. It's a good way to end and think with new intention about words that sound so simple—the Golden Rule—and about our churches, about our lives, and about that myriad of brothers and sisters with whom we share this world neighborhood.

> "For ... we are all one in some obscure way
> that we will never understand
> until we truly learn to love.
> Perhaps ... perhaps if I prayed for the world with
> the same ardor I pray for my own children ...
> I could understand this better." Amen.

Excessive Justice

II Samuel 12:1-15; Mark 15:25-39

Rev. David A. Hollenbeck

This sermon was preached at Calvary Church United Methodist, Arlington, Mass., Feb. 20, 2000.

SIR THOMAS MORE was chancellor of England in 1532 under the disastrous reign of King Henry VIII. It was the time when Henry was married to Catherine. No sons had been born to carry on the monarchy, so he decided to divorce her. The Pope would not approve of this and so the entire course of history was once again changed. Henry broke from Rome and married Ann Boleyn, whom he later beheaded and gave her castle to his next wife.

In the movie, *A Man for all Seasons,* this frightful period of history and the stance of Sir Thomas More are portrayed. Parliament, the lords, the nobles, and seemingly all of England were so frightened of Henry that they gave him their verbal approval. That is everyone except Sir Thomas More who felt Henry was wrong. He did not speak out but he also did not knuckle under to the pressure from the throne. Sir Thomas was greatly respected as a scholar, churchman and human being. Henry was desperate to receive his approval, but he could not get it. He took away Thomas's title and income, put him in prison, had him tried for treason, secured a witness to lie about Thomas, and had him beheaded! All of this happened because Sir Thomas would not sign a national oath saying he believed the king was right in what he did.

At one point, Sir Thomas is talking with one of his last remaining friends, the Duke of Norfolk. The duke is trying to change Thomas' mind and save his life. In a frustrating outburst, Norfolk says to him, "It's ... it's disproportionate, man!" More was not understood. His wife, daughter and friends had a very hard time with his perspective on this matter. His beliefs seemed too strong, even excessive.

We come across many instances in the Scripture where it seems that the point of view, the action and the judgment are excessive. Surely Paul could be called excessive. He was driven in pursuit of converts to the faith. The Pharisees see even the woman who washes Jesus' feet with her tears as excessive. The prophet Elijah won a mighty duel of faith with the prophets of Baal, and Jezebel seeking to kill him. His excessive devotion had consequences!

In one of the most poignant stories of the Old Testament, the prophet Nathan was sent by God to rebuke King David for having Uriah killed in battle so that David could have his beautiful wife, Bathsheba, for his own wife. And the prophet comes and declares David guilty and says that his child, that Bathsheba will soon bear, will die as punishment. All too often the pages of divine justice and love seem excessive from our ordinary human point of view. One Christian commentator says, "To heal individuals or the world itself of great wounds and depths of pain, an equally great cleansing and love are required, such as God alone can give." I suppose one could say that the death of Jesus on a cross was disproportionate, excessive. But that is what God's love and justice sometimes seems to require. It is hard for us to understand and accept. We wonder, "Isn't there an easier way? Couldn't we find a compromise?"

Do you think that ordinary love and action will heal the wounds of decades of prejudice? Excessive love and justice were not applied to our treatment of the American Indian, and the result is over 200 years of disgrace. I feel shame every time I think about it. A great and essentially peaceful people cheated out of their land and turned into eternal refugees.

Excessive love and justice are what is needed to heal the wounds of the great cities of this nation and the world where huge areas have turned into shooting galleries, of drug runners and turf battles among feral children. We do little or nothing because it hasn't touched us yet. Oh yes, there is the occasional inconvenience of a stolen car, but our insurance will provide us with a substitute tomorrow and a replacement in a couple of weeks. We keep hearing about Columbine, but 15 children were killed by gunfire in Washington, D.C. last year and no one lifts an eyebrow.

Thirteen children die every day by gunfire in America and we move our emotions and our lives around this because the kind of justice, and love, and changes that are necessary to put an end to this are too scary, too disruptive, even disproportionate.

We may well want to do something to heal, to help, to make it better, but part of our frustration is that we are not Paul or Jesus or Nathan and we do not see a cause clearly enough to decide like Sir Thomas More that we will give our head for this cause and it will change the course of history. So many causes are complex and we are touched by many, but often we're not sure how to leverage the changes that would be necessary. So we discuss, we preach, we pray and we hope that something will happen tomorrow to make it all better. After all, we are not prophets or bearers of great strength. We are just ordinary people. Yes, we do have strength, intelligence, faith and wisdom that we rarely or never use, but most of the time we feel overwhelmed with the odds against our doing anything to make a difference.

How do we live in a world that needs healing without the gifts to cleanse the wounds? How hard it is to redeem the world when the kids have chicken pox, you've just learned that your brother's wife has cancer, and the talk at the water cooler at work is about the Asian company that is about to buy the business from your employer. In addition, no one has all the answers as to what to do to change things that we think ought to be changed. Well, you're right. No one has all the answers, but perhaps these suggestions will at least give us some food for thought.

First of all, we can all accept our part in some of the ills. For example, many who have thought themselves innocent live in neighborhoods that have at some time been "red lined." Red lining is when the banks have drawn a red line around certain geographical areas that are not to be sold to people of color. Mortgages for people of color simply will not be available in those areas. Every one of us, at least by our silence, have had a part in creating and supporting a racist society, red lining being an example. We do have a role in the continuation of some problems. We pay two or three dollars for an ice cream cone, but the banana that costs only a quarter is harvested and packed by people who live in poverty, have undernourished children and may not even know how to read. We know that physically and mentally an important step toward wellness can be an admission that we need help. As Christian people an important step toward healing is to see ourselves as having a role in the problem. Not one of us is really clean.

Second, I believe it is important to find manageable or even small positive steps that we can accomplish. Concrete actions within our reach are worth our efforts. We cannot tear the phone book in half, but a few pages are within our power. Zacchaeus could give back what he took. Forgiveness is ours to offer to people in our own homes. We can back away from some of the rigid demands we make on others around us. We do touch the lives of others and there are often ways we can improve our sensitivity to them.

Third, I sense a great need for many of us to find some way to celebrate life, to see something good, to be lifted or inspired, to get in touch with the child that I believe still lives in each of us. I worry that the electronic buzz that seems to be sweeping the world will soon be mistaken for fun.

Fourth, within the ordinariness of life there are glimpses, snapshots, of all that is grand, lasting, healing and divine. I knew one woman in Rhode Island who spent one day each week at a special home holding and rocking the babies born with AIDS. I see the faithfulness in those who pass out food in pantries and cook week after week in the soup kitchens. When we moved from one church, one woman said to my wife on our last day, "When you are gone, who's going to hug me?" Within the ordinariness of life there are glimpses of all that is grand, lasting, healing and divine. Look for it, seek after it.

Fifth, (whatever happened to a three-point sermon?) we can look and listen to those who act in ways that we think are disproportionate or excessive and see if we can learn from them. In the movie *Witness* there is a scene where the Amish people in an unarmed confrontation of a man with a gun demonstrate the power of peaceful and determined *presence.* One of the prize photos of the entire last century was of the young man in China standing in front of the tank during a demonstration. We may raise our eyebrows when Greenpeace or other environmental groups become "extreme," but there is often a prophetic voice in their message and we cannot deny that fact. Scores of species and varieties no longer exist. The air and water is so dirty in many places that it makes us sick. In 1998, four out of 10 government agencies were cited for violation of water pollution laws. In another community a storyteller shared that her father had grown up in the South decades ago. He would stand on the city buses when the whites' only seats were full and not take seats of the black riders who were by law supposed to get up and give their seats to white riders. He said, "A law doesn't make a bad thing right!" For his day and time and place, all of this was extreme, excessive.

One of the most excessive ideas of all is God's forgiveness and acceptance of us. A line from the movie, *Babbette's Feast* says, *"Grace makes no conditions and singles out none of us in particular. Grace takes us all to its bosom and proclaims general amnesty."*

The woman in the New Testament story simply kneels and washes Jesus' feet with tears and ointment. No preconditions, she just does it. We may never be in the place of saying or doing excessive things, but we can be sure of this: God's excessive love has set us free to let go of the past and to live fully, even excessively, in the days that are ahead. Those actions that seem extreme, unnecessary, excessive, may be God's way of getting our attention and reminding us that people like you and me are sometimes called on to act out the divine presence on earth and with the whole human family. I believe that God was in Jesus, but is also in all of us. Amen.

Remembering God's Future

Exodus 20:1-17; Matthew 19:16-26

Rev. Jonathan R. Almond

This sermon was preached at Mathewson Street United Methodist Church, Providence, R.I., Nov. 18, 1998.

"I am the Lord your God who brought you out of the land of slavery."

THIS IS THE first word of the Decalogue and prescribed laws of faith and life for the Hebrew people. It is a word of grace. And so it is that grace precedes law. It breaks the division between secular and sacred. It brings all of life into one whole in relationship to God, in the radical presence of God, and in relationship to all our brothers and sisters. God's law claims us to live into the whole range of human relationships. God's law gives us the great gift of responsibility. The demand of the law is to understand what we do with our life in and through the quality of our human relationships. The law begins with the word of grace. *"I am the Lord your God ..."* and then quickly secularizes itself into the whole range of human relationships.

The Hebrews wrote down what they had come to believe. They sensed the power of God loose in creation. They also sensed the spirit of God loose, rumbling around in their history. They were people who knew bondage and were set at liberty to struggle with the sudden physical, psychological and spiritual undertows in their lives. And out of their profound experience with God came specific directions for living, for the humanizing of their lives in community. God's commandments were liberating words which added a whole dimension in life. The word of

God became part of their covenant for living in the world which they sealed with the ritual of blood described in Exodus 24.

Remember after the Decalogue, when the 10 words of God had been given to the Hebrew people, there followed a whole series of specific laws for living in human community. They were given so that the people would love, honor, respect, care and give guidance to one another for the strengthening of human community. We are to know and love one another in human community as we are called to know and love God. The specific laws given in chapters 21-23 are followed by the ancient rite of blood at Sinai in Chapter 24. It is one of the many Old Testament occasions in which, as Gerhard vonRad suggests, God stakes out the covenant claim over all of life. It is a ritual which helps frame an understandable word of God's claim. Blood has two symbolic meanings in the Hebrew Scriptures: that of life which is in the blood and therefore belongs peculiarly to God, and the loss of blood—that of death. The celebration of the radical presence of God is intertwined in this dual understanding of life and death. God's claim finds focus in the call for the people to choose life, that is to live by this covenant with God. This is the quality of life which all of God's people are to seek and live into fully.

Israel often found this quality of life too elusive and too demanding to fulfill, even right from the very beginning of their invasion into the land of milk and honey. Yet, this is the leitmotif of the drama of God's grace in life, moving people to strive to achieve the quality of life which is commensurate with God's future. God's grace at every point precedes God's law. It is not a condition of our relationship to God, but offers us the gracious possibility of reflecting the unconditional love of God in all relationships with our brothers and sisters.

That is, our relationships must reflect God's justice, love and truth. The overwhelming word of our faith is that God won't settle for anything less. God is constantly striving to elicit from us that quality of life which has its fullness in love for God and love for all God's people in the fullness of community. God is after people in a relentless, unceasing search to find and redeem us. This is a word of liberation for the whole human community. God's radical presence in creation seeks to bring human beings into an unbroken fellowship.

The young man described in Matthew's Gospel, who was very rich

(Matt. 19:16-26), was not able to say "yes" to living in radical, unbroken fellowship within the whole human community. That's nothing new, for that is exactly the condition of the Hebrew people when they received this word of God and that's exactly our condition in today's world. The radical presence of God in our lives demands a radical reordering of how we live, causing us to either say "yes" to life and the joys of unbroken fellowship with all our brothers and sisters, or to say "no" to that kind of life and live in the terrible brokenness of our communities. A huge part of the decision for us revolves around the idolatry of money, personal power and prestige in the human community.

Jesus took the commands of God and rephrased them: *"Love God with all your heart and mind and soul and strength; and love your fellow human beings as God loves you."* Jesus was asking the rich young man to say "yes" to God's will and way. The same invitation is given to us to declare our intention to live into God's grace and love in relationship to the whole human community.

T. S. Eliot reminds me of how far from that affirmation of life we really live:

> A cry from the North, from the West, from the East and
>   from the South
> Whence thousands travel daily to the time kept city;
> Where my word is unspoken,
> In the land of lovelies and tennis flannels
> The Rabbit shall burrow and the thorn revisit,
> The nettle shall flourish on the gravel court,
> And the wind shall say: 'Here were decent godless people:
> Their only monument the asphalt road
> And a thousand golf balls."

T. S. Eliot, "Choruses from 'The Rock,'" 1034. III, 2nd Male Voice, *Collected Poems,* Harcourt , Brace and World, Inc. New York, 1970, Page 156.

Still, God in Jesus calls us to say "yes" to God and be in covenant relationship with all people in a life and death affair, where each of us is given the radical commitment to live into the full possibilities of God's embrace.

A young man was murdered in a drive-by-shooting two years ago in Providence. It was just one of many acts of random violence in our city, mirrored by thousands like it in cities across the land each year. Another young man was convicted of the murder and sentenced to life in prison. The significance of this murder and subsequent conviction is that the young man may have been wrongfully convicted. There are flaws in the handling of his case by attorneys, compounded by what looks like a judge and jury rushing to judgment, as well as matters of race and poverty.

The events of our lives lead us into new ways of witnessing for truth and peace with justice and against fear and isolation. Addressing the concerns of this young man has been one such moment. I spoke with the pastors and leaders of the Rhode Island Organizing Project several days ago to ask for our united support to reopen the case of this young man. I don't know if he is innocent, but I believe there is enough evidence and credible voices which say that he may well be innocent which makes it very important to seek a new trial on his behalf. I was asked why we should do this and I said because we must stand up for the sacred worth of every individual and seek restoration of ever person to wholeness and hope.

On Jan. 15, 1989, I was in South Africa at a place called Uppington. Uppington was an isolated town out in the vast Karoo of South Africa. It was a place where there was a penitentiary where the famous "26" had been imprisoned, each charged with murder. None of the people had really committed murder, but all had the misfortune to be in the two-square-block area, sealed off by the police, where the murder had been committed during a demonstration against the apartheid government. All 26 had been rounded up and charged with crimes against the state because of their demonstration and the further crime of murder because of their proximity to the victim. The 26 included a child of 11 years of age and an old man of 87, as well as many young adults. I was in Uppington to enter into relationship with the family members and friends of that community who were suffering the incarceration of their loved one with no sure and certain knowledge they would ever see them again. They only knew that these 26 people had committed no murder and were wrongly imprisoned.

I was part of the group of 12 members organized for this trip to

Uppington with advice such as: "Don't let go of your passport; if you are set upon by dogs, roll up into a ball and cover your head; if there is shooting, lay down quickly and cover your head to protect yourselves from the blows of the night sticks." We met in a small Anglican church into which some 400 people crowded with another several hundred outside the church. Ringing the church on all sides were South African Security Forces which pulled up in truck after truck soon after the worship began. They were armed with automatic weapons, rifles, tear gas and had attack dogs ready to unleash. Believe me, I did not feel secure in such surroundings, except that from within the gathered fellowship there arose such a strength of witness and well-being, through the telling of stories and singing songs of faith, that personal security was soon forgotten.

It was worship in the fullest sense of the word. Our prayers were fervent and our hopes not diminished by the military forces surrounding us. The candlelight grew strong as the evening grew dark, and the light of the Gospel shone in and around our actions. The voices of hope were raised and many more services would be held, until finally the 26 were released to return to their families and into the community which had firmly stood with them through the dark days of captivity.

I tell you this because our ministry in Providence is centered on living into faithful covenant to God by working to build the unbroken fellowship of God's love in community. We stand firm with one another against injustice and seek God's goodness and grace in all aspects of life. A major help in this ministry is through faith organizing. Because our churches have been involved in faith-based organizing for several years, to be neighbors with the whole people of God, we have been able to quickly organize around the matter of seeking justice for this young man. We are seeking new evidence which can be used to reopen his case so that a full and just hearing can be held. This is a justice issue for the people of God to help build the unbroken fellowship of community in our city.

God is calling us to live into the grace of unbroken fellowship where we can share God's love unconditionally. We are reminded of the eternal dimension in all our relationships by living in this way. It is a sad commentary, but in our day and age society often pushes the dimension of eternity out of the center of our living to the very edges of existence, allowing reckless and evil thoughts and deeds to move in. The result is defeatism, anguish, loneliness, despair, and often overwhelming sadness. Sometimes we bring those feelings upon ourselves by our own actions and inability to expand our vision beyond the immediate crises of life. We throw off the power of eternity from our living so that we might follow some momentary illusion of happiness. Then we are left stranded without purpose and meaning. We become godless people when we let our illusions direct our activities. Remembering God's future for our lives requires a daily discipline of talking with God, encountering the living Lord in all of life, and working to build our relationships with one another in the human community.

In a few moments we will be remembering God's future at the table of our Lord. Jesus puts a new twist on this ancient ritual of blood and commands us to remember God's future for the whole human community through the shed blood of Christ. This sacrament helps us to be remembered to one another as we remember God. When we eat and drink at this table we come to behold God and enter once again into the great gift of responsibility which God offers. We are reminded in words from I John, that if we say we love God and do not love our neighbor, then we are liars. Yet, even in this, God's grace is still freely and unconditionally given for each of us to live into the possibilities of being full partners in sharing God's love.

A few years ago a nationwide poll asked, "What word or phrase would you most like to hear uttered to you sincerely?" I was struck by how much the unbroken fellowship of God's people needs to hear three phrases which were most often desired. The first thing people wanted to hear was, "I love you." The second was, "You are forgiven." The third was, "Supper is ready."

How long has it been since we have heard these words spoken to us? "I love you"—God's unconditional love. "You are forgiven"—God's unmerited grace. "Supper is ready"—God's unsurpassed invitation.

Is There Any Hope?

Jeremiah 17:5-10

Rev. Jonathan R. Almond

This sermon was preached at Mathewson Street United Methodist Church, Providence, R.I., Feb. 13, 2000.

THE WORDS OF the prophet Jeremiah come tumbling down through the channels of my mind. I am listening to a dialogue on "Mission and Pilgrimage to the Holy Land." Many at the conference realize how difficult it is to live together if you only see things from one perspective, after listening to a wide range of perspectives on the ongoing conflict in the Middle East. This is especially true after one of the speakers, a Jewish lawyer working for justice on behalf of Palestinian clients, reads a facsimile just received from her colleague in Bethlehem telling of one human rights injustice. There is a problem for an 81-year-old Palestinian farmer trying to get into his field to harvest and plow. The field, recently ringed by an illegal settlement, is inaccessible. Her partner accompanies the farmer on his tractor to the gates of the settlement and instructs the settlers to let them pass to the man's field. No sooner is the farmer working the field than the men of the settlement come to ring the field, each carrying his weapon. Then into the field drive several cars and the occupants get out, armed with clubs and pipes, and proceed to beat up the farmer and the lawyer. They are the women and children of the settlement. The farmer is beaten unconscious and the lawyer receives broken bones. The settlers call for an ambulance because there has been a tragic accident in the farmer's field. The lawyer returns to the field after getting his bones set to retrieve the farmer's tractor only to find it badly vandalized with sugar in the engine making it a total loss. Then the speaker says one of the phrases which sear into the mind, finding lodgment with such clarity, underlining all the barbarity of this report. "The hope of the State of Israel is built on the graveyard of Palestine."

> Lynda Brayer, Society of St. Yves, speaking at the Society for Biblical Studies National Conference, October 22, 1999.)

It is written in the prophecy of Jeremiah:

> The heart is devious above all else; it is perverse—who can understand it? I the Lord test the mind and search the heart, to give to all according to theirways, according to the fruit of their doings.
>
> Jeremiah 17:10, NRSV.

The biblical story of Jeremiah merits our attention as one of extraordinary candor and faith. It is also a story of personal suffering in the context of the deceitful actions of a wayward people and the culpability of the entire nation of Judah in faithlessness. Jeremiah's suffering is at the hands of the religious and political leaders of his own country. There is no happy ending to this story, and this sometimes seems to be very much our story in the postmodern world.

Part of the problem lies in the illusion that the people of Judah think they are masters of their own lives, just as we believe we are masters of our lives and can muster sufficient strength, courage, and energy for any given moment. The truth is that a great many people experience the reality of confusing and destructive forces in their lives without ever being able to do anything about it. This is graphically illustrated by the human drama of a sunken submarine off the coast of Portsmouth, N.H. a few years ago. A faint tapping of Morse code by survivors is heard by the divers who locate the stricken sub: "Is there any hope?" That's the question posed in the curse and blessing statements from Jeremiah in the midst of the confusion and upheaval of our lives. Is there any hope?

Jeremiah's vocation did not unfold as he expected. He first speaks words of warning to his fellow citizens trying to get them to see the hopelessness of sin. The worst of it is that their worship is a mere formality and not given through a heart commitment. Then he is ridiculed, scorned, arrested, rejected and badly treated. He is even placed in the courtyard in Stocks and publicly humiliated. There are those who wanted to kill him. All of this happens at the hands of his fellow citizens.

The perspective we bring to life's unfolding ways can either describe our worst fears or provide us with our greatest hopes. What is required is an honest and authentic understanding of who we are and of whose we are. Kathleen Norris relates a poignant story of two women in a small town on the windswept Dakotan plains:

> "... Two women I know were diagnosed with terminal cancer. One said: 'If I ever get out of this hospital, I'm going to look out for Number One'." And that's exactly what she did. Against overwhelming odds, she survived and it made her mean. The other woman spoke about the blessings of a life that had taken some hard blows. Her mother had killed herself when she was a girl, her husband had died young. I happened to visit her just after she'd been told that she had less than a year to live. She was dry-eyed, and had been reading the Psalms. She was entirely realistic about her illness and said to me, 'The one thing that scares me is the pain. I hope I die before I turn into an old bitch.' I told her family that story after the funeral, and they loved it; they could hear it in their mother's voice, the way she really was."
>
> *Dakota: A Spiritual Geography.*
> Houghton Mifflin Company, New York, 1993, pages 76-77.

Jeremiah makes a faithful witness to a people and a nation who forsake God's goodness and loving presence. The prophet doesn't give up even though his fellow citizens thwart him in every conceivable way. His prophetic words make one thing clear. We are capable of living lives of great dignity and hope in the most calamitous of times.

Mitch Albom has written a richly moving account of dignity and hope in his book *Tuesdays with Morrie.* Morrie is an elderly man who is afflicted with ALS—Lou Gherrig's disease. Morrie relates a wonderful story about a wave, bogging along in the ocean. It is a story of hope told in the midst of extreme pain. The wave is having a grand time rolling along in the beautiful sunlight of a splendid day. But then panic takes hold of the wave as it sees the distant shoreline coming closer and closer with the bouncing waves ahead of him crashing upon its rock expanse. The wave's deductive reasoning quickly swings into action figuring out that it too will crash upon the rocky coast. The wave is joined by another wave who can't help but notice the young wave's panic-stricken expression.

> "It says, 'Why do you look so sad?' The first wave says, 'You don't understand! We're all going to crash! All of us waves are going to be nothing! Isn't it terrible?' The second wave says, 'No, you don't understand. You're part of the ocean. ...'"
>
> Mitch Albom, *Tuesdays with Morrie.* Doubleday, New York, 1997, page 179-180.

We are part of something greater than ourselves. We are God's people, living into God's grace and care. God searches our hearts and knows our deepest desires, fears and needs. And God is present in all aspects of our living, calling us to make a faithful witness to the power of unconditional love and goodness as we live in community with all of God's people. This means no task is too daunting or impossible, including peace in the Middle East. It also means we are able to live in hope through all the conditions of our earthly journey.

Good Shepherd and the Sheep

Psalm 23; Luke 18:3-7; John 10:1-10

Rev. David C. Myers

This sermon was preached at Belmont United Methodist Church, Belmont, Mass., April 28, 1996. The context for this sermon is especially interesting. Some 60 members and leaders of this congregation had been lost to death in a four-year period. New people, young and well educated, were replacing an older group, and the congregation was experiencing both grief for these losses and some anxiety about where the church was heading with new leadership.

SO OFTEN WHEN we think of sheep and shepherds, our religious upbringing takes over and we have wonderful, comforting, soothing images. But I suspect that if we were raised on a farm, the images stirred in our minds about sheep and shepherds would be quite different. Please understand me, I love the 23rd Psalm and the shepherding imagery. As many of you know, I use it often in funerals and also in my devotional life. I also understand the biblical context well enough to understand the power of this shepherding image in an agrarian culture. The pastoral picture of the good shepherd is a valid one, no doubt. Still, I know enough about sheep to know that being likened to one is not at all a compliment. As a matter of fact, being compared to sheep is an insult. Unfortunately, if we buy into the image of God and Jesus being the good shepherd, then we must also realize that we are rendered as sheep. And I'm not sure I like that, no matter how prominent it is as a biblical image.

Our passages this morning are ones of many in the Bible in which sheep and shepherding are the metaphors of God and people. In biblical times sheep were the food of choice and clothes were made from their wool. Add to that tents fashioned from their hides, and it is easy to understand the utilitarian aspects of sheep for that culture. They were essential for survival. Sheep are also mobile and require little care, at least for feeding. It makes good sense why they would be so vital to the nomadic way of life in the ancient Near East.

Scripture is a great repository of allusions to, and stories about, sheep. The story of the Exodus hinges on the fact that a lamb was slaughtered to save God's people. I suppose no Hebrew could imagine Passover without a lamb. Many liturgical stoles carry the emblem of the Paschal Lamb, symbolic of the crucified Christ. And I have here on the pulpit, yet another symbol of the shepherd and the sheep - a hand-carved olivewood statue of a shepherd carrying a sheep draped over his shoulders. But this still can't get around the fact that sheep are smelly, unmotivated and perhaps the most stupid of all agrarian animals. They really do lack character, no matter how much the Bible talks about them. They are, in a word (or two) utterly hopeless creatures.

If this weren't enough, in biblical times shepherding as a vocation wasn't high on the agenda of any self-respecting social climber. Shepherds owned no land, they constantly had to care for the sheep, and they lived in tents wherever grazing land and water could be found. Being a shepherd relegated one to the bottom of the socio-economic ladder. And when you think about it, this contributed to the great scandal of Luke's Nativity story: that the angels' revelation-annunciation would be given to a bunch of grubby hillside shepherds outside suburban Bethlehem. What is even more astounding is that Jesus would call himself the "good shepherd." To his first listeners this must have been a flagrant contradiction in terms. It may even be, in today's terms, an outright oxymoron. And what's worse, if Jesus is the good shepherd that means we are sheep. Not cute little furry lambs that go, "baaaaa," but smelly, stupid, wandering-off animals that need constant shepherding. Nonetheless, there are some powerful images that can expand and deepen our spirituality.

"He leadeth me beside the still waters."

Back in 1988, on my first visit to the Holy Land, we were leaving the beautiful chapel on the Mount of Beatitudes built by Mussolini in the

1930s. We were traveling along the northern shore of the Sea of Galilee heading west to Tabgha, a spot about two miles away that commemorates the approximate place where Jesus both: 1.) fed the 5,000 and, 2.) in John's Gospel commissioned Peter after the resurrection. As we were riding in our tour bus, the guide pointed out a shepherd leading sheep down the hillside along a gentle flowing stream. Edna, our guide, simply commented, "The shepherd is leading the sheep to get a drink of water." I am now convinced she was setting us up. Immediately, the people in the bus joined in a chorus of "Why? They are walking along a nice stream." Edna then told us that sheep would only drink at "still waters and that they would literally thirst to death before drinking waters that were moving." When I got home I did some study on this issue and discovered that indeed she was correct, but it is not so much that they won't drink at troubled or moving waters, but that if these basically dumb creatures do drink at moving waters they will drown. Their anatomy is such that their snout and their mouth are so close that moving water (rapids or waves) would cause them to suck water into their lungs, literally causing the sheep to drown. Suddenly the image of the good shepherd leading us to still waters took on new meaning. God will always go out of the way to lead us past the troubled waters to the safe places where we can safely and peacefully have our deepest thirsts satisfied. Likewise in the 23rd Psalm there is an image of eating.

"Thou preparest a table before me in the presence of mine enemies."

Jerusalem as a city has existed for about 4,000 years, many of them being years of war and great fighting. The city had been destroyed and rebuilt many times as various people and religions have sought to control this city. The passions that exist about this city are enormous. Three of the five world's great religions are Abrahamic religions and claim Jerusalem as one of their sacred cities. In those 4,000 years I'm told that war and fighting have broken out on almost every day of the calendar. Fighting has broken out on each of the religion's high holy days. But there is a sacred time, a time when fighting and war has never broken out. That time is mealtime, when people are "at table." In that region, all the religions and peoples observe mealtime as a sacred time, a peaceful time. Perhaps the reason is that each of the three great religions holds the 23rd Psalm as part of their sacred or most respected writings - "He sets before me a table in the presence of mine enemies." The customs and laws of hospitality that exist in the Middle East - to this day - overcome even the bitterness that exists between enemies when people are "at table." Again an image of the Bible became so much more powerful - the good shepherd goes to great lengths to overcome the stupidity and foolishness of the followers - who will even fight and kill one another over their disagreements.

Well, enough of the good images. Let's get down to the nitty-gritty, because if we consider the good shepherd/sheep analogy, we ought to bristle. In our honest moments, we have to admit we resent the analogy to our being sheep, and of God being a "shepherd" (remember it's an occupation low on the list of most desired jobs). We resent this analogy basically because it is true.

Sheep separate themselves from a flock, not by some nefarious plan to escape, but by simply keeping their head down and grazing from grass clump to grass clump. They graze for hours at a time without regard for anything else - except the grass underneath them. Suddenly, looking up, they realize there are no other sheep around. They have literally eaten their way into a state of lost-ness. We are like this. Most people, left to their own devices, do not want to have "erred and strayed from thy ways like lost sheep ... following the devices and desires of our own hearts." (Isaiah 53:6). And yet we do. Most people we know aren't really good or really bad. People simply forget what is often in their own self-interest. We all need what Scripture calls shepherding. It takes a great deal of truth-facing courage and self-knowledge to understand this.

The good news is this: though the literal analogy of being compared to sheep may be unflattering, we are all in need of a shepherd. (Holding up an olive statue of shepherd carrying a sheep): I don't often use props in my sermons, but I suspect all of you are familiar with this image. I purchased this statue in Bethlehem. It could be the image of the good shepherd leaving the flock of 99 to go and find the one that is lost, and then carrying it back to the flock. That is not a bad image of the good shepherd.

But what prompted me to buy this statute and to be so fond of it is the story told to me about how the shepherds controlled their flocks in ancient times. When a new flock of lambs was born, the shepherd would carefully observe them and pick out the one lamb that seemed to have the most leadership qualities, the lamb that the other lambs seemed to congregate around. Then the shepherd would take that one lamb to a friend, perhaps a fellow shepherd and he would have that friend carefully break one of its legs. The shepherd would then carry that lamb on his shoulders - all day long - while the leg healed. During this time the lamb would literally bond to the shepherd, it would identify the shepherd by his smell and as the one who brought him back to health. The sheep would also know the shepherd's voice because it had heard the shepherd's voice not only with his ears but also through his body from being held so close.

> " . . . and the sheep hear his voice. He calls his own sheep by name and leads them out. When he has brought out all his own, he goes ahead of them, and the sheep follow him because they know his voice. They will not follow a stranger, but they will run from him because they do not know the voice of strangers." (John 10:2b-5).

When the lamb is healed, and incidentally grown up, it is then released back to the flock. Because of its character it enjoys the respect and leadership from the rest of the flock. Because it has bonded so closely with the shepherd who has brought it back to health, it always stays close to the shepherd hearing his voice, and keeping the rest of the flock close as well. I don't know about you but this little statute has given me great new appreciation of the importance of suffering to leadership and being close to God, the good shepherd.

Indeed, God has provided for us the good shepherd. The analogy is true. Like in old times, as a shepherd was not a very popular or highly aspired vocation, neither is our God enormously popular or highly needed throughout times. If God were, would there be fighting, wars, stealing? And the good shepherd will never leave us. Not only will God leave the flock of 99 and go rescue the one that is lost ... well, listen to a final image from Psalm 23:

"Surely goodness and mercy shall pursue me all the days of my life."

No, I didn't make a mistake. A rabbi friend of mine told me that the Hebraic word that we have translated as "follow" is more properly translated as "pursue." It makes an enormous difference. Shadows "follow" you. If you pull a little red wagon, it "follows" you. "Follow," if not a passive word, is at least neutral. "Pursue," on the other hand, is very active. Think of things that pursue you. Bill collectors? The IRS? Do you remember the movie, Butch Cassidy and the Sundance Kid? Remember the scene where Butch and Sundance, those two train robbers of the wild west, are up on a hill lying flat on a rock after running for days from federal agents. They think they have finally escaped their pursuers. Then as they look out over the vast plain, there in the distance, just barely visible is a dust cloud. It is the unmistakable posse that is still pursuing them. And they look at each other and say, "Who are those guys?"

God is like that. God will pursue you, not like bill collectors, not like the IRS, not like a posse seeking to get you, but God, the good shepherd will aggressively pursue you. No matter what you do, no matter what sins you have committed, no matter have far you have "erred and strayed from thy ways like lost sheep, following the devices and desires of (your) own hearts," the good shepherd, "surely" with "goodness and mercy shall *pursue* you - all the days of your life, that you might dwell in the house of the Lord forever." Amen.

Seeing God in the Face of the Enemy

Luke 10:25-37

Rev. David C. Myers

This sermon was preached Feb. 2, 2000 at a Church Conference Center outside of Managua, Nicaragua for a gathering of leaders from the Nicaragua Planning Committee of the New England Conference of the United Methodist Church and la Iglesia de Cristo en Nicaragua as they "conferenced" together for a fresh look at what their covenant means.

I HAVE WANTED TO share this devotional with you for a long time. I wanted to because I so often hear reference to the "Good Samaritan" work we do when we come to Nicaragua. Frankly, I don't know what to make of that statement. Does that mean that we do kind things and give money? If that is all we do, that is not my understanding of this parable. I have a very rich understanding of this parable, but I suspect it is different from how you understand it, or at least how I have heard it explained on my previous eight visits. And sharing our biblical faith is a most important part of what it means to be in covenant with each other.

Sometimes a story can lead us along a path and suddenly take a turn that we weren't expecting. Many of Jesus' parables have a twist in them that lead us to a meaning far more powerful than what we normally think. I believe that is the case with the parable of the Good Samaritan.

When we study the Bible it is important to pay attention to context. And the context is found in the four verses (25-28) that precede the parable proper. There we find a lawyer standing up to test Jesus. He asks what he must "do" to inherit eternal life. The question itself is interesting, because aside from being born, what else can you do to inherit anything in that culture so based on family? At any rate Jesus asks the lawyer to recite the law, religious law. The lawyer does well, saying, "You shall love the Lord your God with all your heart, and with all your soul, and with all your strength, and with all your mind, and your neighbor as yourself." Jesus tells him, "Do this and you shall live." But the lawyer, "wanting to justify himself," asked Jesus, "And who is my neighbor?" Upon that question, Jesus begins the parable.

But before we look at the parable, let's remember to whom Jesus is telling it. The hearer is a lawyer, a member of the privileged class. It is being told to someone well versed in religious law and tradition, and also one who was relatively wealthy. Remembering this is important, because it is his counterpart in the story who is left for dead beside the road. The parable unfolds: "A man was going *down* from Jerusalem to Jericho." Anyone who has been to Israel/Palestine knows all too well that you go down to Jericho from Jerusalem. The two cities are about 19 miles apart. Jerusalem is about 2,600 feet above sea level and Jericho is about 900-1000 feet below sea level, about five to seven miles from the Dead Sea, the lowest place on earth. You literally go "down" about 3,500 feet traveling from Jerusalem to Jericho. There are enormous climatic changes that occur in that 19 miles. I have been to that area in both February and in September, both times there was about a 30-45 degree temperature difference. Jericho is almost tropical; indeed it is known for the wonderful citrus fruits grown there today. Even when it snows in Jerusalem, it will be 60-70 degrees in Jericho. Jericho is like an oasis in the barren desert area near the Dead Sea.

And while Jerusalem was the religious capital of that region, Jericho was one of, if not the oldest, cities in the world. It was along a major caravan route from Egypt to the region now known as Iraq. People who traveled from Jerusalem to Jericho had either of two purposes - to engage in trade, or to take a vacation. But the road to Jericho is a dangerous one. The road borders Samaria, and is hidden in the mountains as it winds its way down to the Jordan River Valley. There would be plenty of opportunity to be stripped, robbed and beaten as the man in the story was. That he was robbed is another indicator of his wealth. We are not told who stripped, robbed and beat him and left him for dead. That is left to our imagination. I think Jesus wanted it that way because our imagination can help define our stereotypes. It could have been anybody, but with the road skirting the border of Samaria, the imagination of the privileged class and that of the lawyer hearing the story would probably assume that Samaritans had done the dirty deed. We are told the man was left "half-dead." We can assume the man had only enough consciousness to see figures pass along the road, but not enough strength to speak or move, and certainly thinking, "if I don't get help soon, I'm going to die."

As the man lies there half-dead he sees a figure "going down" the road. Since we are told the passer-by is "going down" the road, it means he was going from Jerusalem to Jericho. And that figure turned out to be a priest. The beaten man's heart must have jumped. I can almost hear his thoughts. "A priest, he's leaving Jerusalem, he must be going to Jericho for a few days of R-and-R. Surely he has no temple obligations, the laws of cleanliness can be observed, he'll have plenty of time to cleanse himself from my blood before he has to return to the temple. A colleague of sorts, surely he will save me." But the priest doesn't. As a matter of fact "after he saw him," he passes by on the other side of the road. Now this road is not a multi-laned highway. It is more like a cart path. To "pass by on the other side" takes real intentionality as if to go out of his way to avoid the beaten man. The man left robbed, beaten and half-dead had to be devastated.

We want to help the priest get off the hook. As we have told this story countless times, we excuse the priest by saying the laws of cleanliness apply, and for a priest to defile himself with blood would render him unclean for seven days. Well, that would more likely apply if he were going "up the road," going back to Jerusalem and the temple. But in all likelihood, he was going away from the temple for a week or so of vacation. He would be able to cleanse himself before he returned.

Sometime later a Levite comes by. A Levite is a temple assistant, a priest's helper. The man beside the road must have felt, "Well maybe the priest knew the Levite was coming after him and since the Levite is a priest's helper, he surely will take care of me." But the Levite doesn't. He too "passes by on the other side." The man left for half-dead has to be devastated.

We don't like to get involved. In our society people get sued for doing "Good Samaritan" behavior. We always have some fear, some excuse. In 1990, the year before my first trip to Nicaragua, the Reverends Eric Swanfeldt and Richard Black encouraged me to go to Nicaragua to help monitor their historic democratic election. Worried about the potential for violence and thinking of my 10- and seven-year-olds and my wife Debbie, I said to them, "this year won't work." It was a typical clergy excuse, feigning to be too busy. But to myself I was honest and said, "I'll wait until Jesus calls me to do something safer."

Back to the parable. And this is where, I think, we get our most succinct understanding of what Jesus meant as he crafted this parable. A Samaritan comes by. Whether or not it had been Samaritans who robbed and beat the man, the Samaritans were the hated enemy of the Israelites. I don't think there is anything in our time that would rival such a concept of enemy and hatred. The man beside the road had to be devastated, perhaps filled with even more fear and terror. "What will this Samaritan do to me?" *"But a Samaritan while traveling came near him";* I can almost hear the man beside the road say, "I'd rather be dead than be saved by a Samaritan." *"... and when he saw him, he had compassion."* To have compassion means to "bear with" or "suffer with." The enemy, the Samaritan, enters into the suffering of the man who fell among thieves. *"[The Samaritan] went to him and bandaged his wounds, having poured oil and wine on them. Then he put him on his own animal, brought him to an inn, and took care of him." (Verse 34).*

He touches the half-dead man. He anoints him in oil, hoists him on his animal and takes him to an inn, "and took care of him." The next day he gave the Innkeeper the equivalent of two days wages and said to the Innkeeper: "Take care of him; and when I come back, I will repay you whatever more you spend." This Samaritan, this enemy is as extravagant with care as God is with love!

I have some questions. Who do we, as hearers of this story, identify with? While our tendency might be to identify with the Samaritan, that would not have been the case in the first telling. As Jesus told the story to the original hearer, a religious lawyer - that person would identify with the man beaten and left for dead by the road. If that is the case, consider these questions: What does it mean to be brought back to health by your most hated enemy? What does it take to allow yourself to be ministered to by someone you have always detested? And where do we find God in the parable? God is seen in the totally unexpected, undeserved, extravagant help of the Samaritan. It is the supreme example of God's grace. The problem is, is this good news or bad news, particularly if you are a religious lawyer, "trying to justify (yourself)?"

When I visit Nicaragua, I hear repeatedly that we North Americans are here to do Good Samaritan works to the poor in Nicaragua. Don't get me wrong; being a "Good Samaritan" is a good thing to be, but I think we have tended to make a new legalism out of this parable - "thou shalt be a Good Samaritan." While acting like a Good Samaritan is a good idea, I think the real impact of this parable is about where God can show up in our lives. And just what does it mean to have God show up in your life when not only do you not expect it, but actually fear it? And the man "going down to Jericho," a man the religious lawyer could identify with, finds God not in the face of priest, not in the face of a Levite, but in the face of his hated enemy, a Samaritan. Furthermore, it seems to me that the person receiving those "Good Samaritan works" is not a poor person; indeed that person was quite wealthy. Indeed, if we apply generalities of Jesus' culture, the Samaritans would be seen as the poor.

So in the story what we see happening is the poor ministering to the rich. You could even say that we North Americans, given our country's deplorable treatment of Nicaragua in the 1980s with the undeclared war and the embargo against your "Communist country," find you Nicaraguans as our enemy. (Now I don't believe that for a second, but many people in the United States do.)

But there is good news for me in this story, indeed it has been lived out in my life. The poor, the "enemy" has ministered to me. I found God once again in the face of those my country called "enemy" when I came to Nicaragua on my first visit in 1991. From you I learned true hospitality and a pure sense of gratitude. I learned how unimportant material wealth was to my spirituality. I learned more about how the world works, and more importantly, how God works in spite of the world through my visits to Nicaragua. You anointed me and healed much of my brokenness - brokenness of spirit, brokenness or hospitality, brokenness of gratitude. Indeed, I find Christ not only when I am here, but also now I see Christ more clearly when I am at home in New England.

Walter Wink said about this parable, *"The good news is that the bad person helps. When we begin to think that good things can come from bad people, then we can begin to pray for our enemies."* We also can begin to fathom that God's greatness and grace is so far beyond our wildest imagination! "Beyond our wildest imagination" is what being in covenant is all about. We are not here to do "Good Samaritan works" to or for the people of Nicaragua. We are here to be in accompaniment with you. We are here to learn with you. We are here to share faith with you. We may have riches in a monetary sense. Those riches may provide water to the thirsty. Those riches may provide medicine to cure disease. But you have riches that can transform us. You can satisfy our deepest thirst, cure our spiritual sickness. And together we can walk as servants of Christ to spread good news to all our brothers and sisters in the North and in the South.

When I was in high school I remember Alice Drew, a retired schoolteacher, telling my mother: "I like Rev. Travers Smith's sermons; he always leaves you with something to think about." Well, today, I'm going to heed Alice Drew's words of wisdom and try to leave us with something to think about. Who are your enemies? Who are the Samaritans in your life? How can you find God and God's gracious, incomprehensible, extravagant love in those people you despise the most? The story of the man left beaten beside the road tells us that when we can do this we can really understand God's grace. Amen.

Love and Suffering

Genesis 15:1-12, 17, 18; Philippians 3:17-4:1;

Luke 13:31-35

Rev. Dr. Robert O. Stuart

This sermon was preached at Chestnut Street United Methodist Church, Portland, Maine, March 8, 1998.

LOVE AND SUFFERING: the two realities that seem to divide up all this world we live in, pervading the range of experience of our personal lives, our family lives, our communal lives, our global life. Our mind tries desperately to sort them out into opposite corners of our experience. We see them as somehow mutually exclusive and discontinuous: love (over here) and suffering (over there). "Fill us, O Lord with love," we pray; "Save us from suffering," we plead. Yet there is a profound relationship between the two. Much of our love is only increased by the suffering that accompanies it: the love of a great artist who matures through the struggle to realize his or her own art; the fact that children are brought forth into this world with much pain; the witness from life experience that deep bonds of lasting relationship are formed in the tempering heat of pain, stretching, struggle and growth. In such instances, the suffering is so overwhelmed and transcended by the love that is experienced that it loses its power to frighten or convict. As St. Paul reminds us, "The sufferings of this present time are not worth comparing with the glory about to be revealed to us." Yet, the connection is even more profound than that, for love, in its absence, is often what produces suffering; and love, in its presence, is what transforms suffering into something else. This is the great truth of life—

the truth of Easter, the mystery of our faith, the struggle that all of literature, all of poetry, and all of theology attempts to make conceivable to the human mind: love redeems, transforms and overcomes suffering.

The relationship is not in essence a matter of the head alone. There are those who are so overwhelmed by the suffering in the world that they cannot entertain the idea of a God of love at all. For them, the equation is simple: "If God is love, then God would not permit the enormity of suffering I see. Suffering is real. Therefore, God must not be." How many variations of that formula have we heard from those who, in their head, try to master the significance of the magnitude of suffering, which is at every hand?

The resolution of the conundrum is not found by reason, however. It comes in the very presence of God, who crosses the separation, the abyss, and finds us in the very midst of our suffering. God's presence, in the midst of suffering. God's presence, that brings forth the fruits of love, caring, nurturing and healing, is not a matter of the head, but of the heart. It is only in the transformation of the heart into a loving heart, that we discover the true power of love to undo the power of evil and to transform the sufferings of this world into something else.

How can we visualize this profound but complex truth at the center of the Christian experience? What images do we have that can help mediate to the contemporary mind the liberating work and powerful promise of the cross?

There is a story contained in a wonderful little book *The Education of Little Tree,* by Forrest Carter. It is a true story, as the whole book is an account of a Native American boy growing up under the care of his grandparents. He was born in western United States, in the late '20s or early '30s, and orphaned at the age of five or six. The way he had it figured, he was taken in for no good reason by two extraordinary people, his grandparents, who brought him home to West Virginia with them. In the middle of this account of his growing up is embedded this story:

> "One of the ways that folks fished in the middle of the day when fish don't swim and feed but hide in the shadows under the banks, is to lie on the edge of the bank and, very slowly, reach your hand in under the bank. If you move your hand

> slowly enough you can even 'pat' the fish on their sides as they lie there in the shadows in the heat of the day. And if you're very good, you can quickly grasp the fish, and pull it out, and have your lunch."

Little Tree, who was then about 9 years old, was spending the day, as every day, with his grandfather. They decided, in the afternoon, to go fishing in the manner just described. Sensing that his grandfather might want to fish alone and undisturbed, Little Tree decided that he would move up stream a way. He threw himself down on the ground, and had just reached his hand under the bank when, all of a sudden, he heard a dry rattle right next to him. He turned ever so slightly, and there was a monstrous rattlesnake, coiled, with its head raised up a good foot, swaying back and forth, tongue flicking out, eyes fixed on his face. In terror, but not flinching (knowing his only hope lay in remaining entirely motionless) he watched the snake, realizing that he was doomed. Then all of a sudden, a hand came down, right in front of the boy's face. Little Tree's grandfather said, "Stay still!" The hand was rock-solid, and it did not quiver or shake. The snake bit the hand, and the grandfather grabbed the snake with the other hand, and crushed it. Then began the valiant effort to save the grandfather's life.

Little Tree ran off, got his grandmother (who knew about such things), and they raced back up the path to find that grandfather had already lost consciousness. One of the things the grandmother did reminded me of the Old Testament reading for today, when Abraham took all the animals and split them in half, and put them on the altar. She used her skirt to catch a quail. She split it in half and laid it across the gaping X the grandfather had carved in his hand to try to get the poison out, and somehow that bird's body did draw out the poison. (There are sacrificial offerings yet to be made in this world on the altars of our faith and in the face of the wounds of a suffering humanity.)

Against all odds, the grandfather did, indeed, survive. The next day, Little Tree thought to himself that, next to Grandmother, Grandfather must have "kinned" him (that is, counted him kin) more than anyone else in all the world, even more than Blue Boy, Grandpa's favorite blue-tick hound. And out of that great, wrenching experience, the suffering of the past 24 hours, came an overwhelming peace.

Jesus is God's hand, shoved down into our lives, in front of our face, separating us from the confuser, the evil one, the power of Satan, poised to poison and destroy our very souls. Jesus is God's hand, shoved into the middle of our desperate lives, to take the toxins of evil that are so plenteous on this globe, that we might not die. And when we grasp that, then, the good news is not merely some abstract truth but testimony that God's very hand figures into our personal lives, intervening in our most painful struggles, how can we not say, "Thank you, God!" How can we not praise God? How can we not stand up and raise our hands in gratitude? It is overwhelming! It is God's effort to make us kin, to get through our fear and our self-hatred and our sense of unworthiness, so that we might see the power and the simplicity and the wonder of God's love for each of us, by name— a love which takes the toxins of this world out of the suffering of this world, and transforms them as it transforms us. How can we not say, "Thank you, God," and "here is my heart in thanksgiving."

It is hard for us staid, old European folk, especially, to say "Thank you, God" in public. It is hard for us to admit our need, the magnitude of our vulnerability. It is hard for us to admit the overwhelming humility we feel when we see God's hand saving us from our desperate death. So we're going to do it together, in a way that works. I am going to ask the choir to come up and help lead us all in singing a simple, little refrain, into which you can pour your thanks as you praise God for God's hand touching your life, saving your face, from the power of evil.

> Father, I adore you, lay my life before you;
> O, how I love you.
> Jesus, I adore you, lay my life before you;
> O, how I love you.
> Spirit, I adore you, lay my life before you;
> O, how I love you.

Allow yourself to feel in this Lenten season the magnitude of the gift God has given, in offering God's own son to relieve us from the consequences of our sin and our death—not in some distant past or distant future, but in the heat of the summer of our lives, when danger, toils and snares are ever threatening us and putting our very souls at such risk.

Evolution and the Fullness of Time

Jonah 3:1-5, 10; I Corinthians 7:29-31; Mark 1:14-20

Rev. Dr. Robert O. Stuart

This sermon was preached at Wilbraham United Church, Wilbraham, Mass., June 23, 1999.

EACH OF THE readings from the lectionary shares three powerful, concentrated themes. The first is that of "the fullness of time." There are all manners of things in this world for which the time simply comes. The fullness of time implies more than the phrase "It's now or never." The fullness of time implies that something is going to happen, ready or not. David Blanchard recently faced that familiar happening in the world of the theater. He was the director of a play, and facing many impediments; there were many moments when he wondered if there would be enough time to make it come together. But in the fullness of time, things must happen. And when everyone who is in a play lets go and simply lives into the sense that if I do my part, others will do theirs, then somehow it does come together. The idea of the fullness of time captures that double meaning: the very grasp that the time has come, that the time is now, transforms how we live now. In simplistic terms, if there were no deadlines, nothing would ever get done. When we grasp the deadlines that life gives us, we participate in a larger frame of reference and universe of meaning that actually transforms us. We live at a higher level.

The second theme the lectionary readings share is the principle of the power of ordinary people, the power of people on the periphery, to transform the "big fish," those people and groups who think they are in charge, who think they can run things their way forever. Eventually, the power of the people is expressed, and in the fullness of time, when their time for self-expression comes, the people in charge, the big fish, have to make room, have to get out of the way, have to act like it was their idea all along.

The third theme is the key that unlocks the power that belongs to ordinary people: when they see, hear and believe the word of God that is come. When folks "get it." When they respond in faith. When they repent of their disobedience and neglect and forgetfulness, and passionately act out a new way of being because of the liberating word of God that has come to them, then things begin to change. In turn, their transformed behavior transforms the world.

In the Jonah story—so familiar for another big fish story—Jonah arrives at the edge of what was the big fish city in that era. Nineveh, a massive city, bigger even than vast, sprawling cities like Houston, so big it took three days to walk around it. And from the very beginning of Jonah's prophetic ministry, the people on the periphery, the ordinary folks, began to repent when they heard the message that in "40 days the city of Nineveh shall be overthrown." Now some of us may be tempted to think that was simply God's whimsical decision to crush a faithless people. Some of us may be tempted to think that Jonah was talking about a punishment that was going to be visited from outside, in the sense that God was going to intervene and perpetrate a hostile act against Nineveh. In the symbolic language of the Scriptures, however, we have learned to understand this prophetic language quite differently. The prophetic pronouncement of doom is nothing but a shorthand way of saying: Folks, you are so dysfunctional, so irrational, so self-contradictory, that you are no longer a sustainable enterprise. You are destroying yourselves, and if you don't "get it," the consequences of your behavior are self-defeating; change how you behave or your city is going to collapse under its own self-destructive, dysfunctional weight. And the people were so convinced of the message, so thoroughgoing in their repentance, that by the time the king heard it, he had no choice but also to join in the general mood of repentance, put on sackcloth, and change his ways.

In the reading from Corinthians, the concept that the time is fulfilled now, is cashed out this way: the big fish don't matter anymore, for the old form of the world is passing away. There is a new form, a new world order (not to be confused with the political rhetoric of recent years) emerging.

And then, Jesus, in that powerful Gospel of Mark, picks up John's ministry where John left off when he was arrested, saying, "The time is fulfilled, and the kingdom of God has come near; repent and believe the good news." The old order of the world is passing away even now. And he begins to gather the ordinary people, the fisherman, the simple folk and the workers. And he promises to make them something special. Now that phrase in the 17th Verse is very difficult to translate. Every translation comes up with a different rendition, and no one of them is very satisfactory. One scholar suggested that the best translation or paraphrase is this: Jesus is inviting people to join a movement, and he promises them that in the process he will teach them "how to catch the big fish." By the invitation of Jesus, ordinary people are invited into God's transformational process. This transformational process turns ordinary people into an extraordinary presence, into powerful instruments of God's will, even as it empties the power, the big fish, of their power to lord it over others, to dominate and oppress and exploit them. We have seen an example of that in this century in the civil rights movement, when through the power of righteous refusal to submit, otherwise powerless people transformed the balance of power. When people went on the freedom rides, when they participated in sit-ins, when they tried to fulfill court orders to integrate school, and were met with massive and brutal resistance, which was shown on television, then ordinary people, white and black, all over American, rose up until the big fish—President John F. Kennedy, Attorney General Robert F. Kennedy, and later President Lyndon Johnson, and Congress itself—had to respond and support the people's movement for justice.

People of faith know that we are Nineveh—not just America, but the whole globe. And we are in a time that is pregnant with profound spiritual meaning. I'm sure most of you are familiar with the image that Carl Sagan gave the world a decade or so ago, when he compressed what we know about the history of our universe into the yardstick of one year in time. Imagine, for example, if we were to take a white scroll of paper, and wrap it around the whole interior wall space of this sanctuary. The entire length, counting balcony and chancel, would be significantly less than 365 feet. So mapped out on that scale, one day of the 365 days would equal less than one foot, actually about 10 inches. When we compress the whole history of the universe onto this scale, we discover that one second is equal to 500 years. So how do we draw one second on our chart? We have said that about 10 inches is equal to one day. But one day has 86,400 seconds. So one inch would represent 8,640 seconds, 1/10 of an inch would represent 864 seconds. So imagine how short the line would be that represents one second. In the history of human life, then, the last 500 years is represented by a nearly invisible dot! The whole history of human life on this planet, that covers perhaps some two million years, is represented by less than three days—about twenty-seven inches of this vast paper tape. When we look to find evidence of human culture, only in the last 10,000 years are there any remnants of culture other than tool fragments—that is about 20 seconds out of the whole year. Jesus appeared four seconds ago. And the last 500 years, just about the time from the printing press and movable type and the evolution of modern science, we are at one second.

When we talk about the significance of change, we need to put it on that big of a screen. We know, incontrovertibly, that there is a correlation between growth in the size of population, growth in cumulative knowledge, growth in science-based knowledge, and growth in the ability to control in energy—in the amount of energy available to each person. There is a correlation between those factors and discernible, measurable advances in civilization, whether you find those advances positive or negative. We can look back to 1741, when the Reverend Noah Merrick was settled here as the first minister in Wilbraham—1/2 second ago. And in that time, he, the most learned man in the community, participated, along with everyone else (99.99% of the people) in his own food production. We know that until that time, the great revolutions in energy were still very few. From the energy of arms and hands and legs, about 1/8 of a horsepower, humans doubled their available energy to about 1/4 horsepower by the invention of tools. That was about 100,000 years, or on our scale, less than 3 1/2 minutes ago. Not until after the Ice Age, about 55,000 years ago, did humans domesticate animals, and that perhaps led in time to a doubling of the energy available on average.

About 8,000 years ago slavery was added to the energy available to some, which vastly increased what they could accomplish for their own ends. In 1741, Noah Merrick utilized animals, and owned the labor of three slaves. Noah was not alone. All over New England, the clergy as a group owned the largest number of slaves, with over 50 percent of the clergy owning slaves at the time of the Revolutionary War, less than a half second ago. It is only in the last 150 years that our energy resources per person began to change significantly, leaping from about the equivalent of one horsepower each to a huge magnitude more. It is said that since World War II, we have amassed more science-based knowledge than was amassed in the entire prior history of humankind. Science-based knowledge grows exponentially. That is, the more a civilization knows, the faster it is able to learn to acquire new knowledge. Scientists estimate that at present, we are doubling our science-based knowledge somewhere between 10 and 20 years. The next doubling will happen in an even shorter time.

Scientists and religious scholars together are suggesting that we face perhaps the most critical 100 ahead that the human race has faced in its entire two million years on this planet. That if we don't hear the word of God, and understand that if we do not center our social order in moral structures of justice and equity and in spiritual structures of love, and healing, and sharing, we will not be developed enough as a civilization to survive the consequences of the power, the energy, that we have unleashed in our midst. We are the equivalent of a sandbox culture, in which a bully dominates the other children. We, like Nineveh before us, are at that point in which time has run out. We will either hear the word of God, and be transformed by it, or we will bring about the collapse and destruction of the human project on this globe. We are like that farmer on the roof who, when the floods came, first told the policeman who brought warning to evacuate, that he would be all right. He told the second policeman who came—in a boat—with a warning to evacuate, that he would be all right. When the helicopter came to rescue him, the farmer waved the rescuers away saying that " God would take care of him." And then when he wasn't all right, he got angry with God because God wouldn't save him. To which God replied, "Who do you think sent you a warning, a boat, and a helicopter?" To us God says, "Who do you think sent you Jonah, John, Jesus, Martin Luther King Jr.?"

And we have the power of the story, which says that the power of the people on the periphery can make the difference, that they have the power to change how the big fish do business, to turn the world on its head. That's how it happens: when you and I, in response to God's word, say: "No more injustice!" "No more bombs!" "No more battered women!" "No more fear!" "No more stranger!" "No more abandoned children!" "No more neglected adolescents!" "No more expendable human beings!" "No more war!" The time is fulfilled. The Kingdom of God has come near! Do you see it? Do you hear it? Do you have enough confidence in God to act like it? This church can make a difference; it can change the world, from right here, in how we hear and believe.

Christian Stewardship: Partnerships for Growth

Psalm 100; Mark 12:41-44; 1 Corinthians 3:4-9, 10-15

Rev. Wee-Li Tan

This sermon was originally preached at Community United Methodist Church, Wayland, Mass., April 13, 1997. It was later developed and modified for the keynote address given to the Spirituality and Stewardship: Plain Talk for Churches about Money Conference, organized by the Northeast Ecumenical Stewardship Council and held at Wesley United Methodist Church, Worcester, Mass. on March 11, 2000. The NESC consists of representatives from the United Church of Christ, the Evangelical Lutheran Church in America, the Presbyterian Church (USA) and the United Methodist Church. The Rev. Mr. Tan is president of the United Methodist Foundation of New England.

A WOMAN WAS SHOPPING in one of the busy shopping malls that we find in almost every community, and she decided to take a break from shopping. So she entered a specialty coffee shop and bought herself a cup of coffee and a bag of cookies. Unfortunately, the place was packed, so she had to share a table with a man who was reading the newspapers. She put down all her packages, and sat down with her coffee and bag of cookies. Oh it felt good to rest her sore feet! She pulled out a magazine from her bag and began to read as she sipped her coffee. As she reached out for a cookie, she was surprised to see the man sitting across from her reach out and take a cookie too! She was shocked! What nerve this guy has... taking my cookie! She tried to keep calm as she ate her cookie and sipped her coffee. What had happened was troubling her and she could not concentrate on her magazine. She reached for a second cookie - only to see the man reach out and take one too! To make things worse, he smiled at her! She felt flushed with anger, and glared at him. If looks could kill, he would have been dead! Finally, there was one cookie left; she was eyeing it, and so was the man. Before she could do anything, he reached out and took the last cookie! The poor woman was stunned ... The man broke the cookie in two and with a smile, offered her half the cookie. She grabbed it out of his hand and stuffed it in her mouth. The man rose to his feet, picked up his newspapers and with a smile and a nod to her, he walked out. Her coffee break was ruined ... She put her magazine away in her bag, and got up to leave, and then she saw her bag of cookies (moderate laughter). I guess some of you didn't get that (louder laughter). She saw her bag of cookies. She had all along been eating the man's cookies. She had been so upset, because her attitude was, "This is mine, and you are eating my cookies!" And all along, the man's attitude was, "No, no, no, these are really mine, but I am willing to share them with you. ..."

In this day and age, many of us have been conditioned by society to think that what we have is our own - "it's *my* hard-earned money; it's my life; I am a self-made person; I can do what I want with it - it's *mine!"* But like the woman in my story, we've missed the point! It's not ours ... it really belongs to God - God who has graciously shared it all with us ... and we are but recipients of God's goodness and grace.

And that is why it is so important that the starting point of our event today is worship ... (and we thank Rev. Maren Tirabassi for putting together such a creative and joyful worship service). Here we begin our time together by acknowledging that God is the source of all - worthy of our worship and praise! With the psalmist in Psalm 100, we exhort one another to *"make a joyful noise to the Lord, worship the Lord with gladness and come into God's presence with singing." Why?* Because we know that the Lord is God. God is our creator (Verse 6) and more than that—we belong to God *"... for we are his people and the sheep of his pasture."* You and I have the joyful privilege of having a covenantal relationship with God. Let us never forget that.

Stewardship often does not get off the ground in so many churches because we have forgotten all that God has done for us - we are a forgetful people! Let's admit that. So the psalmist reminds us in Psalm 103: *"Bless the Lord O my soul and do not forget all God's benefits, who forgives all your iniquity, who heals all your diseases, who redeems your life from the pit, who crowns you with steadfast love and mercy, and satisfies you with good as long as you live."* Isn't that wonderful? What a litany of blessings! That's who we are as recipients of grace upon grace!

From this starting point, the Christian church has then traditionally gone on to draw its understanding of stewardship from Scripture passages such as Genesis 1:28. Here in the creation story, God, after creating humankind, male and female, sends them forth with the words: *"Go, be fruitful and multiply, fill the earth and subdue it, have dominion over fish of the sea, birds of the air, and over all creation."* This is what I call the *"go, run with it"* model of stewardship. God entrusting creation and all its gifts to us. ... "Go, run with it! Be stewards!" Another popular passage that illustrates this model is Jesus' parable of the talents in Matthew 25:14-30: A wealthy landowner goes on a long journey, and he leaves five talents with one servant, three with another and one with the third servant. In his absence, the first two servants go out and "run with it." They trade with the talents entrusted to them, and they double what they originally were given. The third servant, however, merely buries his talent. After a long time (Verse 19 tells us), the master returns, and demands an accounting from his servants. You know the outcome of that parable - the first and second servants receive the master's praise: *"Well done good and faithful servant,"* while the one who buried his talent is thrown into the outer darkness where there is weeping and gnashing of teeth. Many in our churches understand stewardship in this fashion: God entrusts us with God's resources, and we are to "run with them, faithfully using them, investing them, because the day will come when Christ returns; then we are going to be held accountable." *That's the "go, run with it"* model. This understanding tends to focus on the individual; it is a highly personal and individualistic response to the gifts that we have received from God.

This morning, I'd like us to look at stewardship from a slightly different perspective. You see, stewardship is such a rich and multi-faceted theological jewel. I'd like us to reflect on another facet of stewardship, where instead of a *"go, you run with it"* model as I have just outlined, I invite you to think of stewardship as God's invitation to *"come, join with me."* God invites us to be co-workers with God, partners with God, and also, partners with one another. Here, we are not left on our own devices to *"run with it."* This *"come, join with me"* model if you will, emphasizes the presence and ongoing partnership with God and with fellow believers. We don't go it alone; we are in this together. It picks up the principle that stewardship is not purely personal or individualistic (although there is a personal dimension). Think about the concept of "discipleship." There are segments of the Christian church that place the emphasis on one's personal response: "You have to make the decision." And that is the same thing with stewardship: "*You* go, run with it!" But stewardship understood in a holistic way calls for, no ... *demands*, a corporate and community dimension; that's why there is that call to be in partnership with others. Stewardship is such a fundamental component of Christian discipleship that I would say in fact, that *discipleship is essentially stewardship in action!* And like discipleship, and the Christian life, stewardship cannot be lived out in isolation. We need one another. I invite you to turn with me in your Bibles to 1 Corinthians 3 and let us see this model in action. Many of us are familiar with the problems in the church at Corinth: factions and divisions within the church, groups claiming allegiance to different leaders: *"I belong to Paul ... Apollos,"* each claiming to be spiritually superior. Read verses 5-16:

"What then is Apollos? What then is Paul? But servants ... as the Lord assigned to each." Verse 6 and 7: *"I planted, Apollos watered, but God gave the growth, so neither the one who plants nor the one who waters is anything (read "can claim sole credit for the resulting fruit") for it is only God who gives the growth."* Here we see that Paul and Apollos have different roles and contributions, but they are working together. See Verse 9: *"For we are God's servants, working together... For the one who plants and the one who waters have a common purpose." (Verse 8).* The end result of their concerted efforts is spiritual growth that God enables their efforts to bring.

In verses 10-15, the metaphor changes from an agricultural one to an architectural one as Paul refers to the careful building that each needs to carry out *"according to the grace of the Lord given to me."* (Verse 10). But the concept is essentially the same: each person using their respective God-given gifts, and in partnership with God, works together to bring about spiritual growth.

In this *congregational setting,* we see these partnerships with God and with one another moving the community toward the goal of maturity in Christ, what Paul in Ephesians 4:13 describes as, *"the unity of the faith, the knowledge of the son of God, maturity and the measure of the full stature of Christ."* Likewise, in our *individual walk with God,* God invites us to use our gifts, our talents, our time, our money, all our God-given resources, to grow our relationship with God. This principle of partnership is seen in Philippians 2:12-13. Here Paul writes: *"Work out your own salvation with fear and trembling ..."* But you ask: "Isn't salvation by faith? Can we earn our salvation by our own efforts?" If we stop at Verse 12, then it becomes problematic for us. But Verse 13 goes on to say, *"for it is God who is at work in you, enabling you both to will and to work for God's good pleasure."* Here we have the image of a working partnership. We work cooperatively with God so that God can bring about spiritual transformation and salvation, that is, fullness in Christ. Another word for salvation in the Greek language is *teleios,* "completeness, wholeness, maturity." As you and I seek to grow with God and fulfill the potential that God desires for us, that is stewardship! The life of God in Christ is already ours through faith ... in seed form. Now it is our joyful privilege to work with God in growing this life to fruition.

Anthony Demello tells the story of a woman who has a dream about a shop where she finds God behind the counter.

She asks God, "What do you sell here?"

And God replies, "Everything your heart desires."

So she says, "Well, I'd like peace of mind ... love and happiness and wisdom, and friends, and freedom from all fear." And then she adds, "Oh, and not just for me, but for everyone on the earth."

And then God responds, "You've got me wrong. You see, we don't sell fruits here - only seeds."

In Christ, God has given us the seeds of all these things already (Ephesians 1:3: *"God who has blessed us in Christ with every spiritual blessing in the heavenly places"*), seeds of opportunity, seeds of abundant and eternal life that are ours in Christ. Now we need to grow them into fullness. That's what stewardship is all about. It is about using all that we have - our gifts, our lives, our talents, our abilities, our money and financial resources, the human relationships that God has given to us, friends, families, community—to grow our relationship with God. Stewardship is not so much something we *do* or carry out so much as a becoming/a spiritual transformation as we grow in our relationship with God.

The *"come, join with me"* model of stewardship then is our response to and acceptance of God's invitation to grow in our relationship with God to spiritual maturity through partnerships with God and with one another.

You notice that up to this point, I have not talked much about money, and perhaps there are some of you who are drumming your fingers with great impatience. (I know that the tag line for our conference is "plain talk for churches about money." I'll come to that in a moment.) However, I really believe that once we understand the "spirituality" aspect of stewardship in our conference theme, *"Spirituality & Stewardship,"* the money talk will follow naturally. You do not have to sneak the subject of money into your sermon, or find excuses to raise the topic of giving, financial resources or material possessions. Once stewardship is clearly understood from a theological perspective, and we recognize God as the source of life and all that we have, then the issue of our stewardship of money will naturally, legitimately follow, because people will see that giving is an integral part of growing our walk with God.

Someone has said: "If your goal in life is to find happiness, you're never going to find it - it will be like that illusive butterfly just always beyond your reach. But if you seek God and God's Kingdom (Matthew 6:33), you will find God, and you will experience happiness as a bonus thrown in!" The same is true about money and stewardship. As pastors and key lay leaders in our churches, I know the concerns you have about meeting your church budgets and finding the financial resources to carry out your ministries. But if our focus is just on money and fund raising, or if we're here today just to pick up a couple of tips for raising money, new programs or the latest gimmicks, be assured of this: we probably will raise some money, but that's only fund raising; we will not have gotten to the fundamental basis for stewardship.

So what I urge you to do is teach *stewardship* and *grow your relationships with God.* Help your congregations recognize that holistic stewardship is more than financial stewardship, that it needs to be preached on a year-round basis and not just once a year during the church's financial campaign in the fall. When we do that faithfully, then spiritual transformation and faith-building will result, and people will give. The story about the widow's mite in Mark 12:41-44 that was read to us is not primarily a story about money or giving, although Jesus does refer to her sacrificial gift to the temple treasury. The lesson here is really about this woman's relationship with her God. Her willingness to give with total abandonment was an indication and measure of her love for God, and her dedication and trust in her God to provide for her needs.

In the temple, the people were throwing their offerings (tithes/temple taxes) into a trumpet-shaped receptacle. The larger the coin, the louder the sound. The widow's two *lepta* (i.e. "slim ones" equivalent to one penny) certainly did not make a loud noise. Yet Jesus said, *"Truly I tell you, this poor widow has put in more than all those who are contributing to the treasury." (Verse 43).* What in essence, Jesus was saying was: "Can you hear that marvelous sound? It is the sound, the music that declares complete loyalty, absolute surrender and wholehearted trust in God." Then, and perhaps much more so in our day and age where materialism and possessions have such a strong hold on our lives, our willingness to let go and share of our material resources is a measure and an indicator of our spiritual commitment and our relationship with God. The problem in so many of our churches is not so much a financial one but really a spiritual one! God invites us to transform our thinking about giving, moving us beyond the level of obligation to the glorious heights of spiritual opportunity and service.

A missionary I know tells the story when he was a small boy growing up in Kansas. He would save up his pennies so as to support missionary work in China. Specifically, his pennies were used to buy tires for the Jeep that the missionaries used up in the mountains of China. He would pray daily for those missionaries, and each time he would end his prayers with, "Bless Rev. John, O Lord, and take care of him. Please also take care of those tires, my tires, so that that they will bring him safely to those villages in the mountains to preach the good news." For this little 10-year-old boy, there was no dichotomy between faith and his financial giving. *"Where your treasure is, there your heart will be as well." (Matthew 6:34).*

In the mid 1970s, I had the privilege of working with a missionary organization in Africa. I recall on one occasion when we were working with a local church in a poverty-stricken area in northern Nigeria. After conducting a series of evangelistic services with the local church, the church deacon wanted to give us a monetary gift that was quite substantial for one in his circumstances. As the leader of our team, I thanked him but indicated that his family and his church could probably use those funds. He was indignant at my response, and said: "Why would you rob me of the joy and blessing of giving? We want to be in partnership with you in the work of Christ!" I was deeply humbled by this man's response. When our lives are touched by God's grace and we recognize it, we are set free to be generous people!

The widow in Jesus' day, the little boy in Kansas, that Nigerian Christian, they are all examples of giving and generosity that arise out of a deep appreciation of their relationship with God; in a way, they saw themselves as partners with God for growth. You have often heard it said, "Give until it hurts." But I think it is more accurate to say, "give until it feels good," because in so doing, you are reflecting God's character, knowing that your gifts are touching lives as your own life has been touched by God!

There is a statue of Jesus with outstretched arms outside a church in a city in Europe. During the Allied bombing, the hands of Jesus on the statue had been blown off. After the war, visitors came back to help rebuild the church. When someone wanted to repair the statue, the priest said: "No, don't do that. This statue of Jesus will always serve as a reminder to us of who we are as Christ's church." And he pointed to the words that someone had scrawled on the pedestal of the statue: "You are my hands." And so we are. Jesus invites us to be partners with God, to be his hands and feet, to go forth loving, giving, serving, witnessing, being channels of blessing to a broken world. And as we do so, we grow in our relationship with God and we will help others connect spiritually with God.

There was a funny exchange between a pig and a chicken as they talked about having breakfast together. The chicken suggested, "Let's have bacon and eggs." To which the pig replied, "No way, that's only a *contribution* for you. For me, it is *commitment*!" The question we need to ask ourselves is: "Is our discipleship and Christianity mere contribution of a few dollars when the offering plate comes around? Or, is it a commitment of our whole lives, our time, our money and our energies? Are we willing to give all to be a disciple of Christ?

A story is told about Clarence Jordan, who formed the *Koinonia* commune in the 1950s in rural Georgia. This was a radical experiment where blacks and whites lived together in community. Needless to say, there was great opposition to this community living, and a lawsuit was brought against him. Clarence went to see his brother, Robert, who was an attorney with political aspirations. Clarence asked Robert, "Will you represent us?" To which Robert sadly replied, "I can't ... this will be political suicide!" It is reported that Clarence turned away in disappointment, and then turned back to Robert with these words, "You are willing to follow Jesus up to a point ... and then you stop; you stop at the cross. You are *not* a disciple of Jesus, you are only an admirer!" Friends, are we willing to go all the way? Are we disciples of Christ or mere admirers who are not willing to press on when the going gets hard?

In closing, let me tell you a story about giving that always challenges me in a deep way whenever I tell it. A pastor gave a sermon challenging his congregation to give financial support to an outreach ministry. A woman came up to him after the service and gave him a check for $50, and asked, "Is this OK?" The pastor replied: "If this gift represents you, and represents the quality and depth of your relationship with God, it is fine! It is a beautiful gift." The woman took the check back. She later came back with a check for $100, and asked the same question, "Is this OK?" as she sought for some assurance from the pastor. Again he responded, "If this gift represents you, and represents the quality and depth of your relationship with God, it is fine!" The woman hesitated for a moment, and then took back the check. After two days, she came back with a check for $500. "Is this OK?" To which the pastor gave her the same reply. You could see the tension in her face; she was torn inside. She took it back. She did come back however the next day, and she was beaming. "After much prayer, I have come to the conclusion that this gift represents me. It represents who I am, and I am happy to give it for God's work!" And she thrust a check for a $1,000 into the hands of her pastor. As she came to recognize what God meant to her, she gave accordingly, and joyfully! For now, she knew that the gift came from her heart. It represented who she was and her relationship with her God.

This morning as we have talked about stewardship, as we have heard God's invitation to come and join God and our brothers and sisters in Christ, in partnerships for growth, are we willing to say, "Yes!" to growing our relationship with God? Let us say "yes!" and know the comfort and blessings that come with that assurance that we do not journey on alone!

Pure and Undefiled Religion ...

James 1:17-27; Mark 7:1-8, 14-15, 21-23

Rev. Wee-Li Tan

This sermon was originally preached on Nov. 16, 1997 at Community United Methodist Church, Wayland, Mass. Later it was preached on June 7, 1998 at the Annual Conference of the New England Conference of the United Methodist Church, on the occasion of Rev. Mr. Tan's receiving the Ziegler Award in Preaching.

DO YOU KNOW the story of the woman who prepared a ham for cooking, and she would always cut off the end of the ham? Her husband asked the question, "Honey, why do you do that? Why do you cut off the end of the ham?" Her reply was: "That's the only way to do it! I learned that from my mom, and she told me that whenever you cook a ham, you cut off the end." He said, "Oh, well, let's ask your mom the next time we see her." So the next time he saw his mother- in-law, he asked her that question: "Why do you cut off the end of a ham before you cook it?" And her reply was, "Well, there is this tradition in my family, and my mother taught me that when you cook ham you always cut off the end, and that's the only way to do it right!" "Yes, but why?" "I really don't know, but I am sure there is a good reason for that. My mother is always right." The following Christmas, this man gets to ask the grandmother the big question: "Why do you cut off the end of a ham before you cook it?" And the answer was simple. She said, "My baking pan was too short!"

All of us live our lives following traditions of different sorts. You remember the musical *Fiddler on the Roof*, with that opening song

"Tradition." And while we may not follow tradition as strictly as that main character in the musical, I guess we can say that *in general* our lives are guided in varying degrees by the different traditions we have inherited—family traditions, traditions in our churches, and yes, even traditions at annual conferences. The traditional way of doing something is a safe and comfortable way. We have grown up doing it, it is something that is familiar, and it gives order to our lives—we know it, we like it, we want to keep it that way. Human nature is such that we dislike change for we find security in constancy, in doing things the same old way.

Traditions are good. There is nothing wrong with tradition *per se*—family, religious or other kinds of traditions—but there are some dangers particularly with religious traditions that I would like to mention this morning:

Sometimes a blind adherence to our religious traditions becomes an excuse for maintaining the status quo; it is *business as usual.* We end up not being *open* to God and the leading of God's spirit. What is God saying to us as an annual conference? What new direction is God calling us to move into? What new priorities are we to focus on? What new ways of doing ministry? Or what new structures do we need to enable more effective ministry? All of these can be stymied by a narrow focus on "doing it the way we have always done it." I am so glad that we adopted the report of the Visioning Task Force. Yes, there were changes and modifications, but claiming this vision for our annual conference indicates a *new posture,* one that proclaims our openness to God's leading and our desire to respond to God's challenge to break new ground and move forward into the future—into the new millennium.

The other danger arises when the religious traditions we have inherited and follow become a *means of judging others* rather than a gracious means of helping people connect with God. So we hear people say, "*They* need to live up to our standards! *They* must follow our rules and regulations if they are going to be one of us." That was precisely the kind of criticism that was leveled at Jesus by the Pharisees in Mark 7:5: *"Why do your disciples not live according to the tradition of the elders, but eat with defiled hands?"* Why do they not wash their hands before they eat? The issue here was not a concern for good hygiene or physical cleanliness, but a concern for *ritual or sacred cleanliness:* If you have not kept our rules, then you are ritually *unclean*, and consequently, you are not acceptable to God, and therefore, not acceptable to us.

As religious leaders, the Pharisees had good intentions. We need to realize that. They wanted to interpret the Mosaic Law for the ordinary people. Unfortunately, the road to destruction is paved with good intentions! There is a *fine* line between zeal and fervor for God on one hand, and a self-righteous obsession for religious practices on the other. Jesus criticizes the attitude by quoting the prophet Isaiah in Mark 7:6-8: *"This people honors me with their lips, but their hearts are far from me; in vain do they worship me, teaching human precepts as doctrine. You abandon the commandments of God and hold to human tradition."*

So if we are not careful, we too can so easily slip into this way of thinking and functioning. Listen to this remark by Thomas Erskine who puts it very succinctly: "Those who make religion their God will not have God for their religion." In other words, religion in the sense of our personal or institutional attitudes, beliefs and practices, the rituals that we go through and the traditions that we follow—these may actually get in the way of our relationship with God.

Before I went to seminary, I spent a year and a half working with a missionary organization in Africa and Europe on a Christian ship called the "Logos." One of the ports we visited was Rotterdam in the Netherlands. In the city center, there is a town square that had a statue of a man with outstretched arms, eyes gazing upward to the heavens. What is unique about this statue is that it had a great big hole in the center of his chest! Our Christian guide told us that the statue symbolizes the city of Rotterdam, a city that had lost its soul and its identity, hence, the big hole! He went on to explain that in World War II, Rotterdam was almost totally destroyed by the bombs dropped by the Allied forces. This Dutch Christian went on to add that this statue is also an appropriate symbol or parable of much of the Christian Church in Holland. His perspective was that many Dutch folk profess the Christian faith, but unfortunately, it is a profession that does not translate into a lifestyle that reflects the Gospel. Like that statue, he went on to add, Christianity in Holland lacks spirit or soul. The heart of the Christian faith is missing; it lacks the essence of a true Christian identity. That description could so easily apply to much of North American Christianity. There are many who, in the words of the apostle Paul, "hold onto the form of religion but (by our lives and actions) deny its power." We have religion but we have missed out on the heart of it all, which is love for God and the reality of a vital connection or relationship with God.

James makes the same point in Verse 26 of Chapter 1 of his epistle when he writes, *"If any think they are religious and do not bridle their tongues, they deceive their hearts, their religion is worthless."* The words "religious" and "religion" come from the Greek words, *threskos* and *threskia,* both referring to the outward aspects, the ritualistic elements of religious practice. James is emphasizing the point that these external observances such as liturgy, ceremony and the different postures like kneeling and prostrating, are *in themselves* worthless if one's conduct and behavior—such as the control of one's tongue—is lacking. You are kidding yourself if you think that this is all there is to one's religion!

So, what then is *true* religion? What then is *authentic faith,* that which goes to the heart of the Gospel and represents God's perfect will? In Chapter 1:27, James describes it as *"pure and undefiled religion before God."* He uses the same terms that the Pharisees pride themselves as upholding: "pure and undefiled religion!" But James goes on to make it clear that it is not a ritual purity that comes from a scrupulous observance of the Mosaic Law that counts. Rather, purity of religion, the quintessential element of faith, is that perfect love for God and one's neighbor that results in loving care for the needy (caring for the orphans and widows in distress). Here, James is giving a concrete example. The "real thing," authentic faith, results in holy living when we become *"doers of the word and not merely hearers." (Verse 22).*

A story I love illustrates this point:

> A person searching for answers to life comes up to a rabbi with a question, "How can I live a *fulfilling* life?" The rabbi tells the person to look out through the window. "What do you see?" he asks. The person replies, "I see a single parent on welfare trying to make ends meet; I see youth doing drugs, and people who are homeless and hungry; I see discrimination and exploitation. There is a lot of needy and hurting people out there." The rabbi then says, "Take a look at the mirror, and

> tell me what you see?" The person replies, "I only see myself." The rabbi goes on to say: "That's right. When silver is added to glass, it blocks out the needs of the world and the result is that you can only see yourself."

Likewise, when the silver of wealth, privilege, comfort and complacency is added to the windows of our lives, all we end up seeing is ourselves! We block out the needs of the world. But life is not only lived in here, it is lived out there in the world, and we can never find fulfillment in life until we can begin to see the needs of others and be willing to share our lives with them.

Authentic faith, what James calls "pure and undefiled religion" is not shrinking away from people and things that might ritually taint us. On the contrary, "pure and undefiled religion" will not be content with going through superficial motions in our places of worship, in our churches and yes, even at annual conference; it will propel us out into the world to share our lives through holy living. (See: James 1:27b: *"to keep ourselves unstained by the world.")* It will challenge us to recognize those elements of privilege which blind us to the needs of others. It will challenge us to break through these human traditions and restraints that hold us back, so that we might be doers of the word, setting right the injustices which mar God's world.

An example of this injustice is racism. Last year, the bishop and the leaders in our New England Annual Conference met with staff from the General Board of Religion and Race to discuss the issue of racism and inclusiveness in our conference. It was an eye-opener for some to recognize that racism is alive and well even in the church. In a church that preaches the Gospel of Jesus Christ, which says, "All are equal before God," racism, discrimination and exclusion exist in our midst. Let me share a personal experience that I will never forget; it has left an indelible mark on my psyche. A number of years ago I was a visitor at a worship service in a church where I had never been before. Being a newcomer, I arrived early; nobody spoke to me. I slipped into an empty pew and spent some time in prayer in preparation for worship. More and more people were entering the sanctuary at this point in time; but interestingly enough, nobody sat in my pew! Soon, most of the other pews were filled up, and yet here I was, the only one sitting in my pew! I was beginning to feel a little uneasy; I did take a shower that morning, so that's not the reason! Finally, a woman came by and sat down at the end of my pew (there really weren't any more empty places in that small church). Then the pastor invited the congregation to greet the person sitting next to them. After what seemed like an eternity, she turned to me, looked me over, and then in a measured voice, she said, "H-o-w d-o y-o-u d-o?" I was taken aback by her assumption that because I was not white, I spoke limited English! I confess that just for a fleeting moment, I was tempted to respond in a *Charlie Chan* manner, "ds,lvaslzzcz" (hands together, bowing). But I resisted that temptation, and responded, "I am very well thank you, and how are you?"

Some of you may say: "Oh Wee-Li, you are being too sensitive! That woman, and people in similar situations really do not mean to be racist." But that is precisely the point, they do not mean to! They don't even realize that there is anything wrong with their actions. They can't see that it is racist and degrading! The "silver" of privilege, *white privilege,* has so clouded the windows of their minds and experience that they have no clue what racial ethnic people or people of color have to endure on a daily basis.

The issue of racism and white privilege is one of *power and control* by the dominant racial group as it relates to ethnic minority people. Ultimately, the question is: Is there a *willingness* for people of the majority culture and race to recognize that; is there a willingness on their part to relinquish power and to yield control? In a discussion group at that meeting of church leaders last November, a question was asked, "What is it going to take to have real change?" Some people had expressed pessimism: "We've been talking about racism for decades, but the problem continues. What is going to be different this time?" We all agreed that nothing is going to change until *racism is confronted for the evil it is.* So that people do not make excuses for it such as: "Oh, they're just a little ignorant; they don't mean it. It is only a small matter." More than that, it will take divine intervention! Unless we are willing to allow God to break through into our consciousness, bringing a deep conviction of sin, and allowing God to change our hearts and minds, no substantial change can happen. We need the radical transformation that God's Spirit brings about. We can almost liken it to being "born again," nothing short of a conversion experience! Our revised vision statement for our annual conference begins with "transformed by the Holy Spirit." Let us confess our need for God's Pentecost spirit of renewal and change!

There was a moment in that meeting, which I spoke of earlier, which deeply moved me. It was when the members of the cabinet and the leadership team made a public confession before all gathered, enumerating the different ways in which racism and white privilege had influenced their lives and relationships. When we are willing to confront our racist attitudes and name them before God and the community, then God can do a renewing work of grace.

Another issue that confronts our church, over which there is much disagreement, is the issue of homosexuality. There are many different points of view. The Council of Bishops of the United Methodist Church has made statements on the subject. Groups and caucuses within the denomination have argued their positions, often with polemical language. The church needs to recognize that people have been excluded; there has been a lack of love that has caused much hurt and pain on both sides of the debate. There has been pride and self-righteous attitudes; the church needs to confess to that. Let us remember the reminder that James gives us in 1:26 of his epistle, *"if your tongues are unbridled, your religion is worthless." And again in 1:19f, "let everyone be quick to listen, slow to speak, slow to anger, for your anger does not produce God's righteousness."*

Let us put aside the rhetoric and the name-calling, and labeling of one another that goes on, whether it be "you are homophobic!" or "you deny the authority of Scripture!" just because we hold different positions on the issue. Let us also put aside threats of schism in the church. It is so much easier to give up on people we disagree with, but mature Christian love demands that we persevere and hang in there. We need to work it out in love. And we constantly need to remind ourselves that the traditions we have, whatever they are, have an insidious way of creeping in and forming a barrier between God and us.

Listen to what P. L. Whalberg has to say:

> "The Communists are right when they say religion is the opium of the people, because religion in the sense of devotion

> and loyalty to form and traditions, ritual and patterns of piety may make us feel good while insulating us against a real encounter with God, insulating us from a relationship with God that confronts us with our own sin and shows us the right way to go."

And he goes on to say,

> "Jesus' call to repentance and faith, witness and service is to help us move beyond that." *The Clergy Journal*, May/June, 1991, Page 47.

This morning Jesus says to us, and I say this to myself as well, "you have a fine way of rejecting the commandment of God in order to keep a tradition." I think we need to think about it, each one of us, individually and corporately as a church, as an annual conference. What traditions, *threskia* (religious observances) do we hold that deny God's love? Are we in love with our tradition and our practices and our piety to the extent that they exclude our love for God, and love for one another? That is the danger. James echoes our Lord's indictment of the Pharisees with his call to "pure and undefiled religion," because "pure and undefiled religion" is essentially love in action! Be doers of the word, be doers of love, sharers of love, builders in love, not those who tear down. Be inclusive, not exclusive; welcome, not turn away. How? By the power of the Holy Spirit!

Ten Commandments or Ten Suggestions?

Exodus 21:1-17; I Corinthians 1:18-25

Rev. Dr. Robert K. Sweet

This sermon was preached at Old South United Methodist Church, Reading, Mass., March 26, 2000.

A MAJOR CONTROVERSY HAS been going through the court system in the past year. A judge in Alabama has placed the Ten Commandments on the wall of his courtroom. The civil libertarians argue that the tablets are a religious symbol and have no place there. He argues that he hopes it will serve as one means of bringing the United States back to a basic morality. I ran across a cartoon recently showing some ancient stonecutters hard at work with chisel and hammer. All around them, towering above them, were stacks of stone tablets, presumably already cut and filed. Two priestly looking types are standing at the side. (Maybe Moses and Aaron?) One says to the other, "The legislators and attorneys aren't quite finished with the commandments yet."

Just what are we to do with the Ten Commandments in today's world? William Willimon, minister of the chapel and chaplain to students at Duke University, writes,

> "The commandments are not guidelines for humanity in general. They are a counter-cultural way of life for those who know who they are and whose they are. Their function is not to keep America running smoothly, but rather to produce a

> people who are, in our daily lives, a sign, a signal, a witness that God has not left the world to its own devices."

William Willimon, Pulpit Resources, Jan.-March, 2000, Page 53.

The Ten Commandments come out of the Exodus experience. The Hebrews had been held captive for decades, slaves to the Egyptians. All their life was circumscribed, all their activities prescribed, their entire behavior dictated by their masters. Now they were liberated. Now they were free. How were they to live in relation to this God who had delivered them? How were they to live in relation to one another? As people of faith who had gone through this experience together, a community of people with common history, experience and gratitude, how were they to live out their lives?

The Ten Commandments became the clear and primary answer. The first four commandments determined the way they would relate to the God who had liberated them. The last six would help them relate to one another, not to other nations and other peoples, but to one another. These were promises they made to God, their half of the covenant of liberation. It was an act of gratitude, not an act of petition for acceptance. There is a similarity with a marriage relationship. We know the difference between a nuptial agreement and a marriage covenant. The first ensures that each lives up to the terms of the contract. The second provides opportunities for expressions of love and gratitude. The first lives out of legalisms. The second lives out of genuine love. Why do you bring your wife or husband flowers? Why do you light a fire, turn on the music, and sit reading quietly before the fire? Why do you lean over and kiss your spouse or take his or her hand? Why do you coo over a new niece or nephew? Why do you pick up a toddler and hug him or play with her? I have a four-year-old grandson who rings my doorbell every Tuesday morning. When I open the door he backs up to the other end of the porch, points his finger at me and says, "Go away; I don't like you, Granddad!" (I trust he'll grow out of that one of these days!) It never takes more than a few minutes before we're on the best of terms and he doesn't want Granddad to leave when I have to go to work. But I still love him unconditionally.

Why do we do these things for our loved ones? To fulfill the law? To complete the obligations of marriage or parenthood or grandparenthood?

Of course not. You do these things because you love your partner or that child. It has nothing to do with laws and agreements. It is out of such an expression of the Hebrew people's gratitude and love for God that the Ten Commandments came into being. The first two commandments have to do with placing no other gods ahead of the God of Israel and creating no idols. Except for things like the Oscars and the Emmys, we don't literally create graven images or idols in the 21st century. However, things like money, status and security play a pretty prominent role in our lives. As United Methodists, we are in danger of making idols of things like the Book of Discipline, the Ten Commandments or even the Bible itself. Perhaps the larger question for us ought to be, "What do we do with the Bible in today's world?"

In our denomination, we take pride in a tool called the "Wesleyan quadrilateral." It is designed to help us struggle with tough questions in life. It consists of Scripture, tradition, experience and reason. While Scripture is primary, it is not solo. We believe God expects us to put it all together. Let's try out the Wesleyan Quadrilateral with the place of women in the church. We find certain activities of women in the Old Testament to be an abomination to the Lord that bring about God's anger and punishment without pity. In the New Testament, St. Paul says some pretty derogatory things about women including, "Women should not speak in church." If all we use is the Bible, that puts women, and men who respect women, in a pretty tough spot in today's world.

Let's look at tradition. If we look only to the history of deacons, ministers and bishops in the church, we have to look pretty hard to find any women. Here and there we see them, but not very often before the 20th century. Tradition alone would leave us a church with only male clergy.

Let's look at experience. It's obvious that anyone who takes seriously the history of the church in the last century and a half can see the major impact of women in the church. The women gave birth to the commissioning of women as missionaries. The Women's Division of the United Methodist Church has been at the forefront in issues of justice and mercy, especially as related to women and children, unparalleled by any other organization, secular or religious. We have had the experience of women leading worship, bearing testimony to the Gospel, and leading the way in women's suffrage and civil rights movements. And yet, in 1878 the New England Conference of the Methodist Episcopal Church refused to ordain the Boston University School of Theology graduate, Anna Howard Shaw, simply because she was a woman. Experience was beginning to teach us that there were women in the church who had gifts and graces for ordained ministry just as men did.

The fourth leg of the quadrilateral comes into play with our reason. Given all we know, what we've read in Scripture, what has been our tradition, what we have experienced in the church, and given that we affirm the worth and dignity of all human beings—affirming all people as children of God, regardless of age, sex, ethnic origin, sexual orientation, or handicap—does it not stand to reason, (guess I have to address the men), that we need to be more than simply "nice" and "genteel" to women? Without reason, we would not have Jean sitting here as an ordained elder, or many other women as well. How much poorer the church would be if we were not able to expand our thinking and embrace God's grace for all people!

The freedom given us in Christ causes us to do things that are not always in harmony with society. The Ten Commandments brought the people of Israel in conflict with the culture around them. The ways of God are not always the ways of the world. As the Apostle Paul said, "God makes foolish the wisdom of the world," and "the foolishness of God is wiser than human beings and the weakness of God is stronger than human strength." (I Corinthians 1:220, 25).

May God give us the grace to respond in gratitude, not with the ways of the world, but with the ways of God. Amen.

The Greatest Temptation

Genesis 2:15-17; 3:1-7

Rev. Dr. Robert K. Sweet

This sermon was preached at Old South United Methodist Church, Reading, Mass., Feb. 21, 1999.

IF YOU WERE going to develop a story about how human beings try to be like God, what would it look like? Who would be your characters? What would you have them doing? Well, the author of the oldest writing in the Bible, one of the oldest stories ever told, came up with a dandy!

I won't ask you to raise your hands, but if I were to ask you to identify with one of the characters in this story, whom would you choose? Adam? Eve? The Serpent? God? Which one of these do you think you are most like? I must confess I fluctuate between all of them. At first glance I choose Adam, because he doesn't seem to be as guilty as Eve who tempts him. But then I realize that in the original Hebrew language, Adam and Eve are not separated. The plural is used when the fruit of the tree is eaten. Adam and Eve are inseparable at this point.

Sometimes I feel like the serpent because he was kind of a manipulator. I try hard not to manipulate people, but I know that I am sometimes guilty of doing just that. On the other hand, one scholar considers the serpent the truth teller in the story because the serpent tells the humans that God has not given them the whole scoop. God has not told them all the answers of life. So I like to identify with the serpent when he is seen as a truth teller.

But in my worst moments, I know I want to be like God. I want to have all the answers—or at least make people think I do! I want my way to be right and my interpretation to be the one that is accepted. I'm not comfortable when I am questioned about my assumptions, my actions, or my integrity. I want to be above it all.

The greatest human temptation, it would seem, is to be like God. And the storyteller in Genesis makes the point very well. We see the human race, in the persons of Adam and Eve, establishing their independence over against God. The serpent tells them that only God knows the difference between good and evil, but if they eat of that particular tree in the garden, that knowledge will be theirs as well. So they succumb to the temptation. They eat the fruit. They get the knowledge. But it is not a knowledge that they ever manage very well.

Yes, in the human race we think we have the knowledge of good and evil. Certainly we have been given clarity around some of the good and evil in our society and in the world, but we do not always manage it very well. Our will often clashes with God's will. The Kingdom of God often clashes with the kingdoms of this world.

There's a very interesting contrast between the temptation of Adam and Eve and the temptation of Jesus. In Adam and Eve we have human beings who are tempted to be like God and they succumb to the temptation. But in the temptations of Jesus, we see the one who is like God being tempted to defy the God-given limitations on human life, and he does not succumb. He is being tempted to take the place of the Roman emperor in that third temptation, but Jesus sends Satan on his way, choosing rather, to trust God.

It may just be that our greatest temptation in life is not to trust God, as Jesus did. We may just be putting too much trust in our own systems, assumptions, mores, customs and values. We simply may not be able to let some things go in life, surrendering our own control, and trusting God. When we assume that the ways of the world are all OK with God, then we are not trusting that God has a better way for us to be living with each other and with our environment.

The town of Reading has gotten some pretty unfavorable publicity this week in the area of race relations. The Police Department has been the lightning rod, but the reality is that we live in a society dominated by white values, white customs, white attitudes and white habits. If we are white it is not easy to admit that we are the privileged ones. The minorities in our population know that they must always live with a defensive posture, to one degree or another.

Racism is insidious and endemic in our society. We cannot live in our culture without being affected by racism. When the vast majority of images paint black as negative and white as positive, we cannot help but develop the attitude that white is better than black. And that translates into the ways we deal with one another as human beings. Our language shapes our attitudes.

Thank God my grandchildren will never discover the white sheets of the Ku Klux Klan in the family attic, as I did as a little boy. Thank God that many of the epithets and nicknames that were commonly used for African Americans when I was a child are mostly gone from our vocabulary today. But the newspaper headlines still refer to Black Tuesday when the stock market fell, the black cloud hanging over the city's economic woes, the black mark on the lawyer's reputation. Hold those examples over against Ivory snow, 99 and 44 percent pure, (translate color white), the hymn that says "Wash me whiter than snow, Lord," something is described as pure white. And when you hear someone say that something is either black or white, is there any question in your mind which is positive and which is negative?

We deceive ourselves when we pretend that our attitudes toward all people are alike. We deceive ourselves when we say we are a community without the sin of racism. We deceive ourselves when we treat a higher percentage of people of color one way and people who look more like ourselves another way. We deceive ourselves when we pretend that language does not affect our mind set. We deceive ourselves when we pretend that those of us who are white do not have more privileges in our society than people of color. We deceive ourselves when we believe that racism is absent in our community. We deceive ourselves if we do not think God has a better way for us to live with and understand one another. We are tempted to think we have got it right.

As people of faith we are called to hold up the image of God's kingdom in the world, a kingdom absent of racism, sexism, ageism, and all the other "isms" that exclude people from enjoying the fullness of God's grace. We are the ones called to recognize and lift up the clash between the kingdoms of this world and the Kingdom of God. We are the ones who praise the Lord of reconciliation and peace in our world.

In this Lenten season, we are the ones who are called by God to confess our sins of racism and any system or way of life that keeps people from realizing their fullest potential as children of God.

May God grant us the sensitivity and the humility to see ourselves as God sees us and to trust God to show us the way of reconciliation and peace. Amen.

What's It All About?

1 Corinthians 13, Luke 10:25-37

Rev. Anne Robertson

This sermon was preached at the New England Conference of the United Methodist Church, June 2, 2000.

Back in the '60s, the movie "Alfie" asked the question, "What's it all about?" The song was asking about life in general, but I think it is a good question for the church to ask itself every now and again. What is it all about? What is the one indispensable thing to our faith? That song says: "As sure as I believe there's a heaven above, Alfie, I know there's something much more. Something even non-believers can believe in. I believe in love, Alfie. Without true love we just exist."

I wonder if the author of the song knew he was paraphrasing 1 Corinthians 13 - "without love I am a noisy gong or a clanging cymbal." What is true of life turns out to be true of faith as well. The thing that transforms existence into life, the thing that makes the word into flesh is love. Ask Torah, ask the prophets, ask Jesus ... what's it all about? Love. How very wise and inclusive of God to make the core of faith something, as the song says, that even non-believers can believe in. From Genesis to Revelation that thread remains constant. Love may look different in different contexts, and it may not always be easy to tell what is the loving action and what is not ... but the Bible is very clear that love is the nature of God and therefore is the root from which all righteousness springs. Love is why we were created and why we have not been completely destroyed.

It can sound like a lovely platitude, and we read 1 Corinthians 13 and the story of the Good Samaritan so frequently that we are prone to forget that we are no more adept at applying the teaching than the people of Israel whom the prophets reprimanded, or the Jewish leaders of Jesus' day. We teach that the story of the Good Samaritan is told to answer the question, "Who is my neighbor?" and the answer is: "Everybody, even your enemy." Well, yes, that's the question immediately preceding it. But the question that frames the entire passage is not ""Who is my neighbor?" but ,"What must I do to inherit eternal life?" The answer Jesus gives is "The one who loves like the Samaritan loves." With all due respect to the Four Spiritual Laws and many of our past evangelistic efforts, the answer Jesus gives is just love. Not love as a warm, fuzzy feeling, but love as it is lived out in acts of justice and mercy. Love that can be performed by a Samaritan as well as a Jew.

Have you ever really thought about how scandalous that parable is? Remember that Samaritans were considered heretics. They were the ones with the wrong doctrine and theology, the ones that mixed heathen practices with worship of Yahweh and according to Josephus even dedicated their temple on Mt. Gerazim to Zeus. But it is a Samaritan that Jesus picks as the hero in the story. It's about love, not pure doctrine, says Jesus in this parable. And it is the Samaritan who inherits eternal life while all of those with pure doctrine walk on by. What must I do to inherit eternal life? Lift up the fallen, care for the wounded, love your neighbor. Period. We need to hear the scandal of this message again and again. Love is all that is asked of us. Love God. Love your neighbor as yourself. We need to examine our churches and ourselves and ask what happens and what takes precedence when love and doctrine collide—or perhaps in our context, love and the *Discipline.*

What's it all about? It's all about love, from beginning to end. And just like most of God's people before us, we too have forgotten. There is a wonderful story from the tradition of the desert fathers and mothers who flourished as hermits in the early centuries of the Christian church. The story is told that Abba Lot went to see Abba Joseph and said to him: "Abba, as far as I can, I say my little office, I fast a little, I pray and meditate, I live in peace and as far as I can, I purify my thoughts. What else can I do?" Then the old man stood up and stretched his hands toward heaven. His fingers became like 10 lamps of fire and he said to him, "If you will, you can become all flame."

There isn't a lover on this earth that doesn't know that love is a fire. And it's not a controlled burn, either, deciding to burn here and not there. When someone is completely in love, it burns everywhere and spills onto everything. They become all flame. I think that is what Abba Joseph was trying to say to Abba Lot. It's nice that you have the spiritual disciplines down well, but the real goal of all of it is love, to become all flame in our love for God and for each other. To become the burning bush which will make people wonder that we can burn and not be consumed; that will make people come to us to see what it's all about. To be so completely loving that we don't think twice when we see someone wounded by the side of the road.

When we fail in that, we fail in everything. I came to learn that lesson, as I do most of my lessons, the hard way. I was at work my first job at one of the libraries at Brown University. For about a week, we had been seeing two workmen who were in the library installing an alarm system on all the doors and windows. Toward the end of the week, Thursday to be exact, I started to get that stirred up feeling you get when God is prompting you to do something. And I felt that what God wanted me to do was to stop those two young men and to tell them that God loved them and that I loved them. Well, I was 22 years old, newly married, and I didn't think it would be very smart to stop two strange men and tell them that I loved them. But the feeling persisted. And I persisted to refuse it, searching out work that would take my mind away from it. I succeeded. The end of the day came, the men left, their work completed, and I went home without having embarrassed myself. When I came in the next morning, the library staff was buzzing with the news. One of those two men we had seen all week had left the library the day before but had not gone home. He had gone straight to the Jamestown Bridge and had jumped to his death. He left a note. It said no one loved him.

Oh, people. Can't we ever get it? Can't we manage to remember what it's really all about? While we argue about *Discipline* paragraphs, people are jumping off bridges for lack of love, shooting others because hate rages in their hearts. Can't we get it? Can't we remember? Can't we find it in our hearts to love? Can't we work to become all flame? That is what our faith is supposed to be—a love affair in which we are so engrossed that we become all flame. We forget so often. We get so caught up in our controversies and our beliefs that we start to think and even teach that it's all about doctrine. We are so worried about right belief that we have forgotten about love. God knew we would forget. That is why when God first told us to become all flame, to love God with all our heart, soul, and strength back in Deuteronomy 6. God told us to say it every morning when we get up and every night when we go to bed; told us to talk about it at home and on the road and to write it on our foreheads and the door posts of our houses and gates. It's a ridiculous picture when you really think about. All that graffiti everywhere, even on your forehead. But God knew how easy it was to forget. And we did forget. We forget even now and the world is jumping off bridges and shooting up schools while we sit embarrassed in our pews. Is it any wonder that people stay away in droves?

If we could only remember ... if we could only focus on becoming all flame, consumed with love of God and one another in the way a lover is with the beloved. If we could get to that point, then we could see if anybody still had an interest in refining our doctrine, polity, or theology. I doubt at that point that anybody would care about the issues that currently divide us. I think our concerns would be very different. I think we would stop worrying about who our ministers were blessing and start worrying about who they were cursing. I think we would stop worrying about who people were loving and start worrying about who they were hating. I think we would be so completely consumed in being all flame, fanned by the rushing wind of the spirit of God, that our only concern would be spreading the fire. Christianity was never meant to be a controlled burn. It was meant to be a wildfire.

Square one in the Christian faith and in all of life is love. If you missed it, you've got to go back; do not pass "Go," do not collect $200. Go back to square one and start over. "If I speak with the tongues of mortals and of angels, but have not love, I am a noisy gong or a clanging cymbal. And if I have prophetic powers, and understand all mysteries and all knowledge, and if I have all faith, so as to remove mountains, but do not have love, I am nothing. If I give away all my possessions, and if I hand over my body to be burned, but do not have love, I gain nothing." It's not about whether your theology is correct or whether your doctrine is pure. It's not even about *The United Methodist Discipline.* It is about whether the love of God burns hot in your breast. Love is greater than hope; love is even greater than faith, says Paul. That's what it's all about, Alfie. Jesus was love incarnate, the love of God that had previously been expressed in words finally made flesh. The truth for Christians, Jews, and Muslims alike, is that it is all about love. When people ask us "How do we know what that means?" the answer we give as Christians is Jesus. Jesus is the revelation of God, God revealed, which means love revealed. To know what it means to love, we look at Jesus. Jesus did not spend his time on earth in a lovesick swoon. His love moved him to acts of compassion: healing, exorcisms, feeding the hungry, providing wine, raising the dead. His love sometimes moved him to forceful acts running wild through the temple swinging a whip and turning over the tables of the moneychangers, or speaking out harshly against the hypocrisy and injustice of the religious leaders. Sometimes God's love moved him to violate Jewish discipline, working on the Sabbath, refusing to stone an adulteress, talking publicly with women at wells, and portraying a heretic Samaritan as inheriting eternal life before a priest and a Levite. Finally, his love showed what every good love story has always told us that love is willing to endure pain and even death for the beloved.

> They came to Jesus and asked, "What must I do to inherit eternal life?" "Love," he replied.

Abba Lot went to see Abba Joseph and said to him,

> "Abba, as far as I can, I say my little office, I fast a little, I pray and meditate, I live in peace and as far as I can, I purify my thoughts. What else can I do?"

Then the old man stood up and stretched his hands toward heaven. His fingers became like 10 lamps of fire and he said to him,

> If you will, you can become all flame."

Going Out of Your Mind

Luke 24:13-35

Rev. Anne Robertson

This sermon has been preached within the first month after her arrival in each church to which Rev. Ms. Robertson has been appointed. It was last preached at St. John's United Methodist Church, Dover, N.H., Aug. 1, 1999.

ONE OF MY favorite books for mindless reading is the science fiction parody, *Hitchhikers' Guide to the Galaxy,* by Douglas Adams, probably because it contains one of my favorite illustrations of being mindless. The people of the universe are burning to know the answer to the meaning of life. So, to answer that question, they consult the greatest mind in the universe, a computer called "Deep Thought."

"O, Deep Thought," they ask, "what is the meaning of life, the universe, and everything?" Well, this is a tough question and Deep Thought takes a few thousand years to compute the answer. Finally, thousands of years later, the answer is ready.

"Well?" they ask Deep Thought, "What is the answer? What is the meaning of life, the universe and everything?"

Deep Thought answers, "42."

At first they are stunned and think it is a joke. Then someone suggests that it is a profound answer that can only be understood by discovering what the right question is. They then go off on another wild goose chase after the proper question, which turns out to be—as you can probably guess—"what is six times seven?"

I love that scene because it points to one of the great mistakes of our modern culture; the assumption that technical, scientific knowledge, the accumulation of verifiable facts, is the only sort of knowledge, the only kind of truth that there is. If you're going to go asking a computer about the meaning of life, you deserve to get an answer like "42."

In many ways, we are a culture of the mind. I once heard a statistic that claimed that the most dreaded disease in our culture was Alzheimer's, the disease that takes away the mind. When we think of smart people, we think of those with lots of technical knowledge—scientists, doctors and astronauts. Our generic term for a brilliant person is a "rocket scientist," not an English teacher or musician. It's a bias we have toward the technical and verifiable, and that cultural bias spills over into our faith.

Who are the heretics? The ones who do not think the correct doctrines. It doesn't matter what they have done with their lives; if they express the wrong thoughts, we burn them at the stake. The debate over infant versus adult baptism is often a question of how much one has to be able to understand, and we say someone is a believer when they are able to tell us the right sort of doctrine about Jesus. Most important for our point today is that the battles over Holy Communion, also, have largely been fought over thinking. How do we think about the bread and the wine? Are they literally or just figuratively the body and blood of Christ, and how is that rationally possible anyway?

This morning I would like to invite you to go out of your minds for a while, as I think this passage from Luke invites us to do. I don't want to say that our minds have no value. Church should not be a place where you have to check your brain at the door. But neither should it be a place where only the brain gets to participate. There are other means of knowing, other modes of understanding.

The message of Jesus is not so much about how to think as it is about how to live. It is not so much in the thinking, but in the doing of things that we really understand. Most ancient cultures knew this. The smart people were who? The elders, those who had lived the longest because they had real knowledge, the knowledge that comes from experiencing a lot of life. You know this. If I take a course in sociology, I might say I know about poverty. But that is laughable to those who lived in poverty every day of their lives. *They* know about poverty.

This message is especially important for Communion. Look at the story we read from Luke. Jesus walks all the way to Emmaus with two men, talking about Scripture—heady stuff. It is apparently an interesting conversation, but it doesn't allow them to see Jesus. They walk all that way with the Son of God opening the Scriptures to them, and they haven't got a clue who their traveling companion is. When are their eyes opened? When do they recognize Jesus? When Jesus *does* something, when he breaks the bread. It is only *after* they encounter Jesus in the action of breaking bread, the ritual action that preceded every Jewish meal, that they remember what he *said* earlier on the road.

Don't miss this. For a long time we Christians have tried to talk people into faith. We quote Scripture to them, we explain about the cross, and only after they tell us they believe these things, do we invite them to the actions, "Believer's" baptism, or the ritual meal of Communion where God has promised to meet us. Well, suppose the road to Emmaus is telling us that this is backwards. Suppose we need to encounter Jesus in the waters of baptism and the breaking of the bread before we can even begin to understand Scripture or doctrine!

This notion is a part of our Methodist heritage. Wesley, after his heart-warming experience, fought hard to retain infant baptism and promoted what is called "open communion." Anyone could come to the table. He believed that part of the purpose of the supper was conversion, and thus it was open to everyone. He did not restrict it to those who could recite correct doctrine or could explain what was happening. And he did not restrict Communion to those who had no sin. On the contrary, it was precisely *for* sinners who did not understand. Why? Because Wesley could see that it was in the *doing* and not in the thinking that Christ was to be encountered.

Jesus did not go around explaining the doctrine of grace to sinners. Jesus said, "Come out of that sycamore tree, Zacchaeus. I'm going to have dinner with you tonight." Jesus was always getting in trouble for eating with the riffraff. And it changed their lives. Jesus didn't talk grace, he lived grace. As the sinner was accepted at the table of Jesus and invited to share in a common meal, the sinner could understand the message of God's grace in a way that was impossible for those who refused to come until they were "worthy." It is only *after* an unworthy sinner is invited to eat with Jesus Christ that Scripture comes alive. "While we were yet sinners,

Christ died for the ungodly." Let's go out of our minds and come to the table, not because we understand, but in order that we might understand by meeting Jesus Christ in the breaking of the bread.

And now that we're out of our minds that far, other parts of Communion begin to look a little different, too. Jesus said "Do this in remembrance of me." What does it mean to remember? Most of us immediately think of—what else—thinking. To remember is to go into our minds and think about the past. We might even close our eyes to make sure nothing pulls us out of our minds so that we can try to imagine the shapes, the colors, the places, and see them in our heads. But what does remembering look like when we have come out of our minds a little bit? What happens when you lose something and thinking does not help you remember? Don't you actually go to the places where you have been? You must have done this: "Let's see ... I was in the kitchen," and you go to the kitchen; "and then I walked into the dining room," and you walk into the dining room; "and then I went down the hall ... no, wait a minute. I turned here and went into the bathroom—here it is!" Your memory was enriched by actually doing what you had done before. There are many examples of this sort of thing. Crimes are reenacted to aid the memory of victims or witnesses. Therapists help us reenact scenes from our lives to help us remember and to promote healing.

But these reenactments don't just help our thinking, they allow us to experience the event. This means that by acting something out, not only can we experience a past event again, but also we can experience events where we were not actually present. Have you ever been to a historical site? My house in Maryland was a 150-year-old farmhouse that had been used as a station on the Underground Railroad. In the floor of an upstairs closet was a trapdoor that led down a ladder into a hidden room where runaway slaves were hidden as they escaped to the north. I had read about such places, and had thought about them. I remembered what they were. But to enter that house—to live there—was a completely different thing.

As I went down through the trap door into that room, I wasn't a white lady from the late 20th century anymore. All of a sudden I could feel the tension and fear of a slave on the run. I listened for noise on the road, for pounding on the door and demands to search the house; the creaking wheels of a hay wagon, a gentle tapping on the door, and then a whispered password and the click of a lock. I could almost smell the warm bodies, huddled in both fear and hope, down in that small room. I couldn't walk through that house without being a part of the people who had lived there before me, without remembering in a way that was very different from plain thought.

This is the fuller meaning of Jesus' words—Do this in remembrance of me. Listen to it: *do* this in remembrance of me. Not *think* about me, but *do* this in order that you might remember. And as we do this—as we reenact what happened, not just at the Last Supper, but also at Emmaus and at every other meal with Jesus, the same mysterious thing happens that would happen to me in my Maryland house.

We reach out our hands to receive the bread, and suddenly they are more than just our hands. Suddenly, they are the hands of the disciples in Emmaus who have just recognized their Lord among them. They are the hands of the 12 in the upper room. And it doesn't stop there. Christians have been celebrating the Lord's Supper for almost 2,000 years. My hands are also the hands of St. Paul, of Joan of Arc, of Luther, of Wesley, of Martin Luther King, of Mother Teresa. My hands are black hands and white hands, Lutheran hands and Baptist hands, and they are the hands of Christians yet to be born. They are the hands of sinners and because Jesus also ate the bread, they are the hands of God.

Communion is the *act* that makes us the body of Christ. It is the act that brings us together and unites us across space and time. It is not about how we think as individuals, but about who we *are* as a group. It is about our identity, not about our thinking. It is a way of knowing that is out of our minds. We can't *think* Jesus into our midst anymore than we can *think* a departed loved one back from the grave. Ah, but when we begin to get out of our minds and start to *do*, we experience things that happen in no other way.

When I was a child in New England, my father liked to take me out driving in the snow. As soon as the snow would start, he would call me and we would get into the car and go. It was always beautiful, especially at night, when you could watch the snow dashing into the headlights, curving down toward the car like a sparkling white road that led up into the sky. My father has been dead 19 years now, but he lives and is present with me whenever the snow begins to fall, and I get into my car and drive.

I can think about him, but he is not present in the same way that he is in the snow, or when I read one of his letters or touch something that belonged to him. You know this kind of presence, as I know many of you experience the presence of departed loved ones when you sit in a certain chair, revisit a place, read a letter, hold a picture.

To me, this is part of the mystery of Communion. God is with us always, and Jesus makes a home within our hearts, but Jesus Christ is present with us in a special way when we come to the table, and we are present with each other and with all Christians of all time, as we share this special meal. The others are all here—the Communion of Saints we call it—and they join their hands with ours at the table. We are one body with them, with each other, with God. This act is who we are, the body of Christ—one bread, one body. I don't know that because of a course in theology or because I've thought about it for a long time. I know it because I once joined a slave woman in a secret room and felt a dead man live again on a snowy night. Come with me, out of your minds and to the table of our Lord Jesus Christ. Do this in remembrance of me. Amen.

Too Old to Rebel

John 3:1-21

Rev. Dr. Wilbur C. Ziegler

This sermon was preached at Trinity United Methodist Church, Springfield, Mass. between July 1968 and July 1972, during the time when Dr. Ziegler was the senior pastor of Trinity Church. Issues related to the Vietnam War, drug abuse and misuse, racial conflicts and protests were all prominent during this historical period, and provide the backdrop to which this sermon is addressed. Masculine language has been retained, which was normative for the period of these sermons.

DURING THIS JULY 4TH weekend, and quite properly so, all of our news media—radio, television, newspapers and magazines—are reminding us of the really very radical ideals of 200 years ago, that formed the foundation of what we now call the American Dream. And during this weekend, I think, we are mindful, too, of our forefathers who had the amazing courage and great openness of mind and spirit to accept new ideals. To use those ideals to form a new style of life for this nation that we all love.

I am reminded, as I think of those forefathers, of the style of life of a man referred to in our Scripture reading this morning. He appears there only fleetingly in the life story of Jesus of Nazareth. Remember the words began: *"There was a man of the Pharisees named Nicodemus, a ruler of the Jews; the same came to Jesus by night."* You know, age has given me a whole new perspective of this man Nicodemus. When I was younger I was very impatient with any man who would wait until the anonymity of darkness would come to shroud his movement through the troubled city of

Jerusalem, so that he could go and visit with the radical rabbi, Jesus, and not be recognized by any of his neighbors and friends. But the passing of the years and the experiences that pile upon us, have been softening my judgment of Nicodemus. Is that true for you, as well?

Who was he? Well, actually we have no biographical sketch to use. He appears only three times in the Gospel record, to the best of my knowledge, and each time very fleetingly. However, the parallel history of the day gives us some information that we can use to fill out part of the portrait of this man. He was a member of the council, they said. A ruler of the Jews. He was obviously a man greatly respected by his fellow man. Obviously greatly trusted by those in the same profession. We can assume he was a man of fine character, an honest man; a man of high integrity. He had fine training in some of the best schools of the land. But these were schools that unconsciously or intentionally would have laid great stress on the preservation of the status quo of his own day. They would have looked upon the conventional as sort of sacred, as God-given, to be preserved at all costs. And anything new, any new idea, any new custom, any new tradition would have to fight its way into acceptance against an authority and against tradition that had stood unquestioned for generations of time.

But that night Nicodemus came to Jesus. He came with a memory about some of the others of the Sanhedrin whom he had left behind. In all probability, I would imagine, he could hear in his memory, the angry, heated words that had been spoken as the Jewish Council considered this radical rabbi. They were outspoken in their resentment of his strange ways, his very questionable teaching—in their eyes. They resented the way he would disregard tradition and authority. He had no respect, it seemed, for them. You remember the harsh words that he (Jesus) heaped upon their heads on a later occasion, which the council used to justify their feeling that he lacked respect for their authority. There were even some, perhaps, who early on had seen Jesus as a danger. They had already spoken that it was very important to discredit Jesus, if at all possible, in the eyes of his followers. That would probably silence him. And if that didn't work, then they would need to silence him permanently—Jesus and all those associated with him! Perhaps, after all, his teaching is like a disease, and if we allow it to infect our religious life, then our religion will be destroyed. So he (Jesus) needs to be cut out.

It was against this backdrop that there was a man named Nicodemus, a ruler of the Jews; the same came to Jesus by night. I see two characteristics in Nicodemus that are needed in the people of God in this day and age, long centuries later—200 years after what we call the birth of our nation. I see two characteristics of Nicodemus that stand out for me, although there are likely many others of value as well. But I want to lift up two.

First, he was a man of courage. I didn't used to see this. But it is there. Because I have come to realize that only a fool is unafraid. It's the man of courage who sees the danger, is fearful of it, respects it, and yet for the sake of life or truth or high principle will act, and even will risk everything for that sake. He was a man of courage. He came to Jesus. He risked his life in coming.

Nicodemus appears very briefly on two other occasions. He is there in the seventh chapter of the Gospel of John, where the Pharisees have reached the point where they are plotting the death of Jesus. And suddenly when they feel they have reached agreement that he must die—no matter how they do it—he has to die. He must be silenced somehow. Suddenly, one of them, Nicodemus—the one who came to Jesus by night— stood and asked, and this took courage, "Does our law permit us to pass judgment on a man unless we have first given him a hearing and learned the facts?" Can you sense the stunned silence that his words must have brought? The anger, the response: "Are you a Galilean? Are you one of his disciples? Maybe we had better include your name with his!" But he stood up and asked a question that needed to be asked. There is a third time, when he briefly appears in the 19th chapter of John, when it's all over. The crowd has deserted Jesus. Most of his disciples have run away to save their own lives. One of them has betrayed him. Another has publicly denied him. Jesus was put on the cross and he died. He was an utterly defeated man. It's over! It takes some kind of courageous fool to identify with defeat. Joseph of Arimathea, asked if he could have the body of Jesus to bury him in his own tomb. Then we read that he was joined by Nicodemus, the same who came to Jesus by night, who brought spices. They wrapped the body in linen and put it in the tomb. Nicodemus was a man of courage. I have no doubt about that.

But the second characteristic is perhaps more important. Nicodemus was a man who kept himself always open to the truth. In spite of the pressure of tradition, in spite of the pressure of authority, in spite of the pressure of the teachings of the years, Nicodemus—among all in the Sanhedrin, the council there, was willing to recognize the voice of God speaking through this strange man from Nazareth. All around him the others ridiculed him. Now what school did he (Jesus) go to? He wasn't even a rabbi. He was a carpenter wasn't he? And he's trying to teach about God? He's from Nazareth, I understand. Where does it say that a prophet will come out of Nazareth? This is ridiculous! But not to Nicodemus. He heard something when this man Jesus spoke that moved the deep places of his heart. He was open to hear what God spoke, wherever and whenever God spoke. The only thing that Nicodemus was fearful of was that for him it might be too late. He realized that he was pretty well along in years. How can a man be reborn when he is old? To put it another way, he thought of all the things that would probably be changed by the teachings of Jesus. "I'm too old to rebel, aren't I?" Do you remember in that great book, *The Desert Fox*, later made into a motion picture, where Field Marshal Rommel, some of the other generals and other leaders of Germany realize that Hitler in his madness is leading Germany and the whole world to destruction. Hitler somehow has to be stopped even if it means taking his life. Rommel is sent to talk to the beloved General, Field Marshal von Rundsted, to enlist his support and aid. Rommel tells von Rundsted all they plan to do. Von Runsted's answer to what he hears is, "I'm too old to rebel."

Well, I can identify with that. But, it is not a matter of years. It's a matter of a frame of mind, the outlook on life. I think as we advance in our years, we recognize the ring of familiarity in that phrase, "I'm too old to rebel." We all resist change. There is so much security in things being the same, day-in and day-out. If you don't believe me, talk to the junior high school youngster, who graduated from junior high this spring. Next fall he is going into that strange place called, "senior high." Or talk to the senior high grad who is looking forward to college, and yet recognizes that this is a whole new experience, and that he has lost the security of the day-in and day-out comfort of being at home. Or, speak with the college grad who is ready to launch out on a career, or the adult who finds his job has been canceled or that he has to change a career. For the high school graduates who graduated this spring, it is predicted that in their lifetime, in their profession, if you want to call it that, those high school grads will change jobs five times, on the average, before they finally retire. All this is unsettling. We don't like change. This is us as individuals. But it is also us as a nation. And that is what I'm concerned about on this July fourth, as we think of the nation. The whole nation resists change, as well, even as we as individuals do. And yet changes come and some of them are glorious. It's new and it's wonderful! Very positive changes.

I'm indebted to an editorial that appeared in *The Catholic Observer*, a couple of weeks ago, that listed a few of these things. For example: do you realize that more people are involved in the political life of this nation now than ever before? And more want in all the time; the blacks of the nation; the young people of the nation; the ethnic groups of the nation; the vast silent majority; everyone is involved in politics now. That's new! That's good! Second, for the first time in history, the most powerful nation in the world has been forced to abandon a war because a large enough segment of the population has decided the war is immoral. That's new! And it is really good, isn't it? The third thing they listed is that black leaders have been elected to public office in cities and legislatures clear across the nation, here and there. And the glorious thing that is happening is that their leadership is sane, is moderate, is reconciling, and utterly capable. That's new! That's good! The last thing *The Catholic Observer* listed is, that religious concern among young people is higher now than in the last 50 years. Now I hasten to say that that religious concern may take on some weird and bizarre shapes and forms. But you cannot deny that religious concern is there. That's new. That's good.

So change comes. And some change we welcome with great joy! And yet even in the midst of it we recognize that there has to be so much more. I do want to lift up one thing. I'm speaking as only one observer. You don't have to agree. Maybe you will have seen something else that I didn't see. But as I look upon this land, yours and mine, I see a spirit sickness, here. I don't know how it appears to you, but it appears to me that we have lost something, a degree of compassion—one for another—in this nation. It is revealed in symptoms that you see every once in a while so starkly in front of you that you can't escape. It is only a symptom, and yet behind it is the disease of the spirit—a lack of compassion. I was reading in the paper (I think it was only yesterday morning) a story about a hundred or so people on Boston Common, men and women, mostly well-dressed, old and young, who had gathered around a public water fountain. On the edge of the fountain, an alcoholic, a drunk stood waving his wine bottle, proclaiming to all who would listen to him, that he wasn't afraid. He had served with the Marines at Guadalcanal. He was afraid of nothing! What did the crowd do? They reverted back to the days of ancient Rome when they put human beings out to fight wild animals. They began to egg on the alcoholic, saying,

"You're a coward!"

"No I'm not!"

"Why don't you climb the fence, then? Leap into the pool. Go ahead."

A couple of ladies collected some money together, a few dollars and some change.

"We'll give you this money if you'll do it!"

And the poor soul, in his alcoholic state of mind, climbed the steel fence and launched himself into the three feet of water and wallowed around in there, while the crowd cheered.

God help us! This lack of compassion that you see every now and then. I'm not saying it's rampant. Yet I see it often enough that I'm concerned about what is behind the symptoms— a spirit sickness. There is no doubt about it that we are all shocked and horrified with the murder of the 16-year-old lad, so close to this church, in fact, just down the street. Yet isn't it strange that even as we are shocked by that, as I talk to people I haven't heard much of an expression of how tragic it is that a 16- year-old boy would lose his life. I have heard a lot of anger about police protection, lack thereof, and all that sort of thing. And even as we are shocked by that, we don't like to remember that our own shells and bombs daily, almost daily, lay waste villages in Cambodia, Vietnam. We don't like to look at the fact that there is a murder of the spirit that takes place under a welfare system that robs people of dignity and self-worth. I'm talking about a lack of compassion. There is a spirit sickness in the land that has to be changed. Is it too late? No. It's not too late to rebel! But like Nicodemus we have to hear the word of God, and hear it where others are saying it is not being said. They said: "You won't hear it in that insane rabbi, that so called rabbi, who is really only a carpenter from Nazareth. That's not God speaking." But Nicodemus listened, and he heard the voice of God.

I'm only one. But I hear the voice of God speaking in the youth of the land. I'm not talking about that tiny segment of young people who are the extreme in terms of their militancy and their willingness to destroy the culture and everything else. I'm talking about the vast majority of young people in this land, who, whether you realize it or not, are deeply concerned for their nation. Deeply concerned. They don't march. They don't shout. But there is something inside their souls that troubles them. We have a troubled generation of young people. I spent five days, a couple of weeks ago, at a conference entitled, *"The Family and Church in a Chemical Comforter World."* The outstanding speaker of that conference, no doubt about that, was a Dr. Helen Nowless, professor of psychology at Rochester University. A year ago she was sent under a government grant to more than 35 college campuses across the country to investigate usage of drugs on these campuses and to somehow give an understanding, an interpretation of what is happening. When Dr. Nowless was speaking to us at that conference, there were some *basic* things that she was telling us. I was expecting to go to that conference and come back with a whole list of things that we could do to treat the young person addicted to drugs. I came away realizing that all the psychologists, all the sociologists, all the experts in the field that had been brought into to speak to the church were saying to the church: "Do your thing." Your thing is to transform society. Your thing is to transform human beings. Your thing is to create and help human beings to be themselves. To be free. To stand up with a sense of their own dignity and their own worth as individual children of God. Dr. Nowless went on to say: "Don't be afraid of your young people. They are not asking us to *give up* social values. They are asking us to *live up* to those values. They have accepted the basic values of life that we claim to adhere to: a) the dignity and worth of every individual as a human being; b) to have a meaningful social relationship between one human being and another human being; and, c) "that institutions are here to serve mankind and not to have humankind serve the institution," as David (Purdy) said last week. Dr. Nowless concluded by saying, "Young people expect us to help create a society where people's basic goodness can emerge in attitudes of confident expectancy and compassion." Think of that! Well, my generation is afraid of its young people.

But don't be afraid. It's not too late. Too late to rebel, too late to change this nation? Oh, no! For as Jesus said, when the Spirit of God is received, wherever a man has the openness of a man like Nicodemus, whenever a nation has the openness of the spirit of a man like Nicodemus—to hear God, then we begin to change. And out of that change emerges a basic goodness of human beings with an attitude of confident expectancy and compassion. It is not too late! This nation is only 200 years old. We have all the future ahead of us. But God can only do it through us. That is both the ecstasy and the agony, isn't it?

The Message for Life

John 13:1-17

Rev. Dr. Wilbur C. Ziegler

This sermon was preached at Trinity United Methodist Church, Springfield, Mass. at some point between July 1968 and July 1972, during the time when Dr. Ziegler was the senior pastor at Trinity Church. This sermon predates wide cultural concerns regarding gender inclusive language, and the narrative reflects that.

DO YOU REMEMBER the story of a man who bought a mule from his neighbor? The mule seemed perfectly strong and healthy in every way. And yet when the man brought the mule back to his own farm, for some strange reason he couldn't get the mule to work. He hooked the mule up to a plow and the mule simply would not pull. He hooked the mule up to a wagon and again the mule would not move. Once in a harness, he simply would not budge. One day, a particularly exasperating day, the former owner dropped by to see how the mule was working out. The new owner said: "I was going to bring him back to you. I've never been so disgusted, so frustrated by a mule in all my days. He is absolutely stubborn. I can't get him to move. I've harnessed him up to a plow, a hay rake and a wagon and he just won't budge. In fact, I've got him hitched up to a plow right now. Look at him. He just won't budge."

The former owner sized up the situation and said to his friend, "Let me show you what to do."

The former owner walked over to the mule, picked up a piece of 2x4 lying nearby, raised it over the mule's head and brought the stick down just as hard as he could on the mule's head, nearly breaking the wood. The mule stood there a bit dazed. The former owner said, "Git up!"

The mule began to move, pulling the plow. The neighbor said to the new owner, "You see, you've got to get his attention first."

Well, the ancient message that I want to reaffirm this morning is so important and so vital to the fullness of our lives that it seems to me that it needs that kind of startling prelude. I don't mean that I'm going to belt you over the head with anything, but it needs that kind of introduction. Something that gets us completely awake, totally alert, so that we know what we are listening to. It reminds me of a recent experiment they were running in the U.S. Navy when they were trying to figure out a warning system for their submarines. They had been using flashing lights, horns, sirens and all the rest to announce emergencies. For some strange reason, after a time these warning signals were not really paid attention to in the fashion that they should have been. Then they devised something utterly new and wonderful that really got attention. I happened to be talking with one of members of the crew on a submarine where this experiment was conducted. After they had been under the water for a number of days, and out at sea for several weeks, all those men alone on the submarine, the technicians experimented with the new warning system. The warning system consisted of the sexiest female voice that they could find. When an emergency arose, the button was pushed, but instead of lights flashing, horns and sirens sounding, they simply heard this lovely girl's voice echoing throughout the submarine: "Attention, all men. There's water in hold number three." And he said, "It was amazing how quickly that lovely voice in the submarine got instant attention!"

Well, of course, I'm only fooling about that. But this message for life that I'm talking about really ought to be somehow preceded by trumpets, the wailing of horns, the pounding of drums, by something that makes us stand on tip toe because it is so vital to the lives that we live today. It needs some sort of sound, some event so startling that, ah, but, of course, it was such an event like that introduced such an idea.

Can you see that cross standing on a hill? Can you see his body hanging there bruised, dirty and bleeding; twisting and writhing in pain that is beyond all endurance? And that man Jesus hangs there because one friend betrayed him. He hangs there because another friend openly denied that he even knew him. He hangs there because other friends fled for their lives and left him utterly alone. And he's there because some people could not face the security of their own little world being threatened by a whole new measure of life. He's there because thousands of people shouted out their allegiance only a few days before, but now at the moment of testing, they stood absolutely silent. The good people—they let him die. Many others just couldn't care less. They have their own problems. "Let him take care of his." He is there because of prejudice, because of selfish concerns, because of cowardly evasion of responsibility, and because of willful choosing of evil. His whole being, hanging there, is a glorious demonstration of love beyond all human measure. It proclaims the glorious, triumphant, thrilling, exciting good news of the Gospel of Jesus Christ: *God loves you! God loves you! God accepts you just the way you are!*

It's almost as if a voice cried out, "Now hear this!" And there it is: *God loves you!*

Now there are two things about that good news which leap out at me that I want to bring to your attention this morning. The first is this: That God loves you and accepts you just the way you are. I mean it. You don't have to put on your best clothes and your best manners. You don't have to use correct language when you are talking with him. You don't have to use spiritual makeup to cover over the blemishes of your Christian soul. He loves you and accepts you just the way you are.

Can you remember the most recent time in your life when you met a person for the first time and every instinct within you proclaimed that this was a person whose friendship you wanted to treasure? And do you remember when you met him how carefully and alertly you maneuvered the opening conversation, so that you only revealed that part of yourself that you were sure would be acceptable to that person? You would reveal only that part and no more. As I was writing this, I was reminded of the fact that I had the privilege, a little more than two years ago, of sitting next to Nicholas Katzenbach. At that time he was the Attorney General of the United States. We had met just before the graduation exercises of Northeastern University in Boston Garden. For a space of about 10 minutes, as we were waiting to go outside for the graduation program, we were sitting side by side in a small room. We had a chance to talk together. I think this was probably one of the most important people in government I've ever met. I was surprised by the gentleness, the humility, the shy hesitancy of this man who so courageously, just months before, represented the federal government in the South during the days of the most dangerous racial crisis. Do you remember that? Well, he and I talked together about subjects of succeeding importance. We began with the weather. It was a hot day. Then we moved to considering and talking together about our families. I remember he had a boy in school. That boy didn't know what he wanted to do even though he had only two more years of college to go. And then we moved to matters much more personal to him.

I remember saying to him, "It must have been awfully tough waiting for confirmation of your appointment as Attorney General." You remember the president waited quite a while before he announced that Katzenbach would move up from Assistant Attorney General to Attorney General.

His response to me was: "No, it really wasn't that bad. I was too busy. You know," he said, "I had never dreamed of being attorney general nor of being in government, in government service at all. I always thought I would be a schoolteacher of some kind. But a strange fortunate series of circumstances of being in the right place at the right time had brought me there."

That's the way the conversation went on. As I remember it now, I remember how very careful I was of wording my sentences. How conscious I was of saying exactly the right thing. I wanted so much to be accepted by him.

But now we are talking about being accepted by someone much more important, much more powerful. We're talking about being accepted by the Lord God Almighty, the creator of the universe, the source of all life, goodness and love. The amazing thing is that God does accept us just as we are. Accepted without going through any hoops to make sure we say the right thing at the right time. There's a wonderful scene in the New Testament that has always moved me. It took place in the upper room. The Feast of the Passover is on; it's the Last Supper that Jesus is to spend with his disciples. And before it begins, you read these words: "Jesus knowing that he had come from God and was going to God, took a towel and began to wash their feet." You and I looking into that room, you could say to me,

"Which one of those men is Jesus?" Which one is God like?

You'd probably look at that great big, tall, strong-looking fellow and say: "Is that him?"

"No, that's Peter."

And then you'd look at the rest, up and down the table, and there is a man who looks alert, very successful type of person, "Oh, there he is sitting between those short fellows."

"No, that's not Jesus. That's Matthew, the tax collector."

"Oh. Well, which one is Jesus?"

And I'd say to you: "There he is. He's that man down on his knees, with the towel on his shoulder, washing their feet."

And you'd say: "You're kidding me. You mean that's Jesus? That's what God's supposed to be like? Unbelievable!"

"No, I'm not kidding. That's what God is like. That's God. The utter acceptance, this kind of compassion for people. That's God."

So, you see Jesus earlier in his ministry, when the adulterous woman is thrown at his feet, and he's supposed to pronounce the sentence of death. But he just doesn't do it. He lifts her to her feet and sends her on her way a renewed person. There's that moment when he talks to the dishonest tax collector and convinces him that he ought to change his whole life. The tax collector knows he can't live this way anymore. Jesus' compassion, his acceptance of people —the discouraged, the lonely, the insincere, the sick, the ugly—the absolute acceptance of each person, the object of his love, just the way they are, that is the way of God.

So, I'm saying that the first thing that comes booming out at us as we are brought to attention by that stark cross on a hill, is the demonstration of the fact that God loves you; God accepts you just the way you are. In a moment, after you've digested this thought, you say to me,

"That's fine. That's good. But is nothing required of us?"

Now, that's the second thing I want to talk with you about, very briefly.

Do we have to make a response? Oh, yes! We have to make a response. Because we feel this love within us, we are compelled to respond. There is something deep within us that drives us until we really do respond. Do you remember Lloyd Douglas's book, *The Robe*?

Remember how he tells us of that time in the life of Marcelus, when he becomes attracted to Jesus. He follows him, listens to him, and then he determines to change his whole life. He's going to be one of Jesus' disciples. He writes a letter to his loved one in Rome. He tells Dianna what has happened to him, how he has found Jesus, how he has listened to him—this wonderful man that Jesus is. Remember her reply? She thinks it is wonderful that he has found Jesus, but then she says,

"What I feared was, that it might affect you. It's a beautiful story, but let it remain so. We don't have to do anything about it, do we?"

Do we? Yes, we do. That's just it, we do have to do something about it. We are called to accept his love, not as an emotional experience, but as a transforming, empowering experience. Whenever men have accepted the compassion, the concern, the caring, the love, the acceptance of themselves by Jesus, they have been compelled and empowered to become new people. They find themselves hearing the voice of this man, Jesus, saying, "You can't live this way anymore." Leave it as a story, if you want to. That's your privilege. Millions have done just so. And God's love has been gladly squandered wholesale on these people. But accept God's love, accept his concern, compassion and acceptance of you just the way you are, and you have to become one of those who is concerned, who is compelled to offer in return our compassion and acceptance of our fellow man.

I see it as if we were reading the stage directions of the great human drama of life. And you turn the page for the particular act of this particular day. At the top of the page there are these stage directions. And it says: "Blare of trumpets, pounding of drums, sound of horns, and a loud voice proclaiming, *'God loves you, accepts you, just as you are, even so you are to love and accept all others.'"*

And so the drama goes on today, tomorrow and forever more.

Index of Themes

AFFIRMATION / INCLUSION

CHRISTIAN LOVE

CHRISTIAN RESPONSE TO THE SOCIAL ORDER

HOLY COMMUNION

LENT / EASTER

JOY / LIBERATION

MISSION

RESTORATION / RECONCILIATION

SEXUALITY

STEWARDSHIP

Index of Scripture

HEBREW (OLD TESTAMENT)

NEW TESTAMENT